GRAMMAR IS IMPORTANT

GRAMMAR IS IMPORTANT

A Basic Course

A. W. McGUIRE, B.A.

IRWIN PUBLISHING
Toronto, Canada

ISBN 0–7725–5009–3

29 30 31 JD 87 86

FOREWORD

From many educational, social, and business groups in all parts of the country has come the demand that students entering secondary schools have a good knowledge of English grammar, including correct usage. A knowledge of English grammar is recognized as a prerequisite to satisfactory work in English composition and literature, and of great value in the study of a foreign language. Its usefulness in social intercourse and in business goes without saying. We are pleased, therefore, to publish this text, which deals with the essentials of English grammar in a straightforward manner and with no intermingling of other phases of language work.

Throughout the book grammar is presented in a simplified way, so that pupils need not be discouraged or confused by its difficulties. Each new point is carefully explained, and followed by suitable exercises. A special feature of the careful organization of GRAMMAR IS IMPORTANT is that only constructions which have been already taught are used in the exercises in the first ten chapters. Other important features are the emphasis on the functions and relations of words, the inclusion of oral exercises, and the avoidance of formal definitions, with only a few exceptions. We know of no other book in which detailed and clausal analyses are so well developed.

The subject matter usually prescribed for the junior high school grades is covered in this text. A suitable division might be: Chapters I–V (Grade 7); Chapters VI–XIV (Grade 8); and Chapters XV–XVIII (Grade 9). As the sequence of topics has been very carefully worked out, it would seem advisable for grades 7 and 8 to adhere to the order in which they are presented. In grade 9 it is anticipated that the teacher will select freely for review purposes from the lessons for the earlier grades. From the abundant exercise material to be found throughout the book, the teacher of any of the grades should feel at liberty to select or omit in accordance with the ability of his class. Review exercises are provided, beginning on pages 47 and 164; there are useful appendices beginning on page 175; and a detailed index starts on page 179.

THE PUBLISHERS

Table of Contents

CHAPTER I: ANALYSIS

CHAPTER II: PARTS OF SPEECH

CHAPTER III: VERBS AND COMPLETIONS

CHAPTER IV: KINDS OF SENTENCES

CHAPTER V: REVIEW

CHAPTER VI: NOUNS AND PRONOUNS

CHAPTER VII: VERBS

CHAPTER VIII: SPEAKING AND WRITING CORRECTLY

CHAPTER IX: NOUNS

CHAPTER X: ADJECTIVES AND ADVERBS

CHAPTER XI: SIMPLE AND COMPOUND SENTENCES

CHAPTER XII: COMPLEX SENTENCES

CHAPTER XIII: CLASSES OF CONJUNCTIONS

CHAPTER XIV: CONJUNCTIVE PRONOUNS

CHAPTER XV: VERBALS

CHAPTER XVI: DIRECT AND INDIRECT OBJECTS

CHAPTER XVII: ACTIVE AND PASSIVE VOICE

CHAPTER XVIII: GENERAL REVIEW

APPENDIX

INDEX

CHAPTER I

ANALYSIS
Subject and Predicate, Modifiers, Analysis of Sentences

Before You Begin

Before you begin the study of grammar from this book let us talk very briefly about the subject and the way it is presented here.

Great care has been taken to arrange and explain the various topics so that you can easily grasp them. Try to learn each part thoroughly, because that will help you to understand what follows. Each day you will see that you are making progress, and you will have the satisfaction which comes from learning something well.

To learn grammar you must use your reason more than your memory. If you reason out each point, your memory will easily retain the various facts and rules.

A knowledge of grammar will aid you in reading, in writing, and in speaking. People judge you by the way you speak, and you cannot afford to make a poor impression. *Watch your English* is a good slogan.

Subject and Predicate

In these two-word sentences, try to decide why each word is used.

Grass grows.	Pupils study.
Men work.	Flowers bloom.
Children play.	Horses run.
Wolves howl.	Leaves fall.
Birds sing.	Lightning flashes.

You will notice that the words in each sentence have different uses. One word names the person or thing

1

spoken about, and the other tells what is said about that person or thing.

The part of a sentence which names the person or thing spoken about is called the SUBJECT; the part which tells what is said about the subject is called the PREDICATE. In each sentence the subject is a NAME WORD and the predicate is an ACTION WORD.

EXERCISE I

(a) Study again the sentences on page 1 to see how the work of the subject differs from the work of the predicate. (b) Compose ten sentences with two words in each. Place a single line under each subject and a double line under each predicate.

Example: Fish swim.

Helping Words

Compare these sentences with those on the preceding page.

Grass grows *quickly*.   *Diligent* pupils study.
Honest men work.   Flowers bloom *early*.
Children play *here*.   *Frightened* horses run.
Hungry wolves howl.   *Dead* leaves fall.
Birds sing *sweetly*.   Lightning flashes *suddenly*.

In each sentence you see one word which is not on the preceding page. This word is connected in thought with one of the other words. Read each sentence several times to see the connection, and give the use of the new word. Note, for example, in the first two sentences:

Quickly tells how grass *grows*. It is connected in thought with *grows*.

Honest describes *men*. It is connected in thought with *men*.

Words which work with subjects are SUBJECT

2

HELPERS. Words which work with predicates are PREDICATE HELPERS.

EXERCISE 2

Write the following sentences, and place a single line under each subject and a double line under each predicate. Decide whether the third word is a helper of the subject, or a helper of the predicate.

Example: Wild flowers bloomed.

1. Snow melts easily.
2. Rusty hinges creak.
3. Pigeons coo softly.
4. Owls screech loudly.
5. Happy people sing.
6. Ripe fruit spoils.
7. Flies dart about.
8. Good diamonds sparkle.
9. Tortoises walk slowly.
10. Small bells tinkle.
11. Dim lights flicker.
12. Tired workers rested.

EXERCISE 3

Write the following sentences, and place a single line under each subject and a double line under each predicate. Connect the subject and its helper, or the predicate and its helper, with a curved line.

Examples: Warm air rises.　　　Time passes quickly.

1. Small lambs bleat.
2. Winter lingers here.
3. Fierce gales blew.
4. Trains travel swiftly.
5. Early birds twitter.
6. Rain falls everywhere.
7. Crickets sing shrilly.
8. Large snowflakes fell.
9. Indians lived there.
10. Sunlit waters glisten.
11. Dust whirled around.
12. Pioneers worked hard.

EXERCISE 4

(a) Without using any word twice, compose sentences with three words in each, using only the following words:

eyes, lions, fly, brave, steadily, savage, cry, sparks, sick, hoarsely, upward, wilt, clocks, quickly, children, frogs, closed, died, tick, roar, soldiers, croak, sleepy, flowers.

3

(b) Using the sentences which you have written in (a), place a single line under each subject and a double line under each predicate. With a curved line connect the subject helpers with subjects, and the predicate helpers with predicates, as shown in Exercise 3.

Modifiers

In grammar we call the helping words MODIFIERS. The word *modify* means *to change*. When you become well acquainted with modifiers, you will see that they do, in a way, change the meaning of the words they modify. For example, notice in these sentences how the modifiers change the meaning of the words they modify.

Hostile natives appeared. *Friendly* natives appeared.

When the modifier is connected in thought with the subject, it is called a MODIFIER OF THE SUBJECT. When it is connected in thought with the predicate, it is called a MODIFIER OF THE PREDICATE.

Write the sentences which follow. Place a single line under the subject, a double line under the predicate, and connect each with its modifier as you did in Exercise 4. In addition, separate the subject and its modifier from the predicate and its modifier by a vertical line.

Example: Many flags | fluttered gaily.

1. Light canoes glide along.
2. Big boys played roughly.
3. Wealthy people spent freely.
4. Small fish swam about.
5. Happy days arrived again.
6. Good seeds sprout quickly.

7. Bright stars twinkle nightly.
8. Wild geese passed overhead.
9. New cars run smoothly.
10. Gallant men perished there.
11. Friendly people live here.
12. Much snow fell then.

Complete Subject and Complete Predicate
Bare Subject and Bare Predicate

In Exercise 5 you divided each sentence into two parts, with the subject and a modifier in one part, and the predicate and a modifier in the other part. One part of the sentence is called the COMPLETE SUBJECT, and the other part is called the COMPLETE PREDICATE. The underlined words are the BARE SUBJECT and the BARE PREDICATE, and are the main parts of the complete subject and the complete predicate.

EXERCISE 6

Write the sentences which follow. Divide the complete subject from the complete predicate by a vertical line. Place a single line under the bare subject, and a double line under the bare predicate.

Indicate each modifier by the use of these marks:

Modifiers of the Bare Subject [ ] *Modifiers of the Bare Predicate* ( )

Example: [Dry] wood | burns (well.)

1. Slender leaves stirred gently.
2. Dull days passed slowly.
3. Brave rescuers toiled ceaselessly.
4. Thin ice breaks easily.
5. Young partridges hide quickly.
6. Heavy bombers flew high.

7. Kind doctors spoke softly.
8. Hungry animals eat fast.
9. Dark clouds passed over.
10. Fancy skaters performed gracefully.
11. Most birds migrate regularly.
12. Noisy trains thundered by.

Analysis of Sentences

The separating of sentences into parts, which you have been doing in Exercises 5 and 6, is called ANALYSIS OF THE SENTENCE. The word *analyse* means to *separate into parts*. Learning how to analyse sentences is one of the most important steps in grammar, and is necessary to the study of more advanced work. It helps us to understand the meaning and structure of sentences. It also shows the uses of words in the sentence.

EXERCISE 7

Analyse these sentences with lines and marks as you did in Exercise 6.

1. Strong winds blew continually.
2. Heavy frosts came early.
3. Huge breakers rolled ashore.
4. Healthy children sleep soundly.
5. Tropical storms come suddenly.
6. Educated people speak correctly.
7. Some pupils read fast.
8. Honourable men answer truthfully.
9. Welcome news travels rapidly.
10. Many spectators cheered lustily.
11. Old people walk slowly.
12. Timid rabbits scampered away.

Graphic Analysis

The separation of a sentence into parts by the use of lines and marks, such as you have done in preceding exercises, is called the GRAPHIC ANALYSIS of the sentence. As your markings show clearly the complete subject and the complete predicate, it should not be necessary to continue using a vertical line between them.

Short Modifiers

The shortest modifiers you will meet are: *a, an, the.* You will learn more about these words later. When occurring in a sentence, they should be separated from other modifiers, or from the subject.

Examples: [The] [crooked] road winds (around a hill).

[The] animal turned (swiftly) (on its pursuers).

[A] call [for help] came (from the disabled ship).

Word-Group Modifiers

A modifier is often a group of words, which is called a WORD-GROUP MODIFIER. Sometimes a word-group modifier can be replaced by a single word which has the same meaning.

Examples:

Pupils study *in this room.* Pupils study *here.*

Boys *with good manners* behave properly. *Mannerly* boys behave properly.

Nurses move about *with care.* Nurses move about *carefully.*

Events *of importance* happened *at that time.* *Important* events happened *then.*

Very often a word-group modifier cannot be replaced by a single word because there is no word which conveys the exact meaning.

Examples:

Smoke *from a dozen chimneys* curled upward.
Scientists experiment *in many ways.*
Grain *of various kinds* grows there.
People travel *for different reasons.*

Study each sentence above which contains a word-group modifier, and decide on its analysis. This will show you that some word-groups modify subjects and some modify predicates.

EXERCISE 8

Select each word-group modifier and tell what it modifies.

1. The buds of trees open in the spring.
2. The rope slipped from my hand.
3. Lights from many ships gleamed in the harbour.
4. The car crashed through the fence.
5. Snow fell from the roof with a thud.
6. Clouds passed over the moon.
7. A load of hay upset in the lane.
8. The marble in that mantel came from Italy.
9. A lake without a name nestled among the hills.
10. Long icicles hung from the roof.
11. Purple violets grew in the ditches.
12. All eyes turned toward the speeding plane.

Building Sentences

It is helpful to build up sentences and then by analysis to separate them into parts again. Study carefully the sentences of each of the following three groups, and analyse each sentence orally.

1. (a) Ducks fly. (b) Wild ducks fly. (c) Wild ducks fly over the lake. (d) Wild ducks fly over the lake in the fall.

2. (a) Friends came. (b) Friends of my father came. (c) Friends of my father came to our house. (d) Friends of my father came to our house yesterday. (e) Friends of my father came to our house yesterday for a visit.

3. (a) Birds sing. (b) Small birds sing. (c) Small birds sing sweetly. (d) Small birds sing sweetly outside my window. (e) Small birds sing sweetly outside my window in the morning.

EXERCISE 9

Add to each short sentence by using one or more of the word-groups listed below, and then analyse your sentences orally.

Example: Steak sizzled in a hot pan.

Bare Subject — steak
Bare Predicate — sizzled
Modifier of the Bare Predicate — in a hot pan

1. Steak sizzled.
2. Accidents happen.
3. Pupils play.
4. Memories linger.
5. Opportunities come.
6. Trains arrived.
7. Buildings toppled.
8. Mercury expands.
9. Flowers wilt.
10. Flags waved.
11. Water flows.
12. Stars twinkled.

of childhood	at half-mast	on every highway
on time	to everyone	for self-improvement
at the station	on rainy days	under the bridge
in the basement	in a warm room	through a large pipe
in dry weather	in a thermometer	on public buildings
in a hot pan	in a cloudless sky	during the earthquake
in our minds		

9

Aids in Analysis

Work in analysis will be easy if you understand and remember the following points:

(1) Words and word-groups work together in a sentence to express a thought.

(2) Word-groups modify subjects and predicates, and in this way resemble single-word modifiers. Sometimes these word-groups seem to point out rather than describe.

(3) When we analyse, we separate a sentence into its parts, and give each its proper name.

(4) Before starting to analyse a sentence graphically or in writing, do the work mentally. Read the sentence carefully to see its meaning and its parts.

(5) Remember that the subject is never in a modifying word-group.

(6) In your study of a sentence, form the habit of asking questions.

Example:

A brilliant star appeared nightly in the western sky.

The question, *What is the statement about?* shows the subject, *star.*

The question, *What words describe the star?* shows the modifiers of the subject, *a* and *brilliant.*

The question, *What word tells what the star did?* shows the predicate, *appeared.*

The questions, *Appeared when?* and *Appeared where?* show the modifiers of the predicate, *nightly* and *in the western sky.*

(7) Modifiers of the predicate generally answer the questions *How? When? Where?* or *Why?* Each answer gives a separate modifier. Two answers to the same question give two modifiers.

A Study of Analysis

(a) Study each of the following sentences and try to understand the analysis which is shown.

1. Hail pelted (against my window) (in the night).

2. [Pretty] [little] flowers grew (along the stream).

3. Children [in the cities] play (in the parks) (during the holidays).

4. [The] names [of candidates] appear (on the ballots).

5. Columbus landed (on an unknown shore).

6. [Wild] animals prowl (through the jungle).

7. [A] [noticeable] change [in the weather] occurred (during the night).

8. [Several] lines [of customers] stood (outside the door).

9. Rain fell (steadily) (for several hours).

10. [The] girls [at our school] skip (on the walks).

11. Pebbles [on the shore] glistened (in the sunshine).

12. [A] [tame] squirrel comes (to our verandah) (in the morning) (for food).

13. Winds [from the ocean] blow (toward the land).

14. [Thirsty] men looked (longingly) (at the water).

15. [An] avalanche [of snow] slid (over the cliff).

(b) Copy each sentence without showing the graphic analysis. Now close your textbook and analyse each sentence graphically. Check with the text to see how high your score is.

Written Analysis

In previous exercises you have done graphic analysis of sentences. It is useful also to be able to analyse sentences in writing and without the use of lines and marks. This is called WRITTEN ANALYSIS.

Example: Heavy rains fall there frequently.

> *Bare Subject* — rains
> *Modifier of the Bare Subject* — heavy
> *Bare Predicate* — fall
> *Modifiers of the Bare Predicate* — (1) there (2) frequently

EXERCISE II

Analyse each sentence in writing.

1. Rich samples of ore came from the mine.
2. The trip down the river lasts about three hours.
3. Statesmen from many countries assembled for the conference.
4. The bells of the church rang merrily on Christmas Day.
5. Our holidays at the cottage passed quickly.
6. A devout group of pilgrims landed on the New England shore.
7. Threatening thunder rumbled through the sky.
8. Boys with toboggans scrambled up the hill.
9. A bewildered bird flew against the window.
10. Jolting old cars rattled over the rails.
11. Great bales of raw cotton lay on the warehouse floor.
12. A car with a flat tyre thudded over the pavement.
13. The shortest day of the year comes in December.
14. The boys camped by a lake during the summer.
15. The winning team cheered heartily for their opponents.
16. The youngest pupils of the school ran to the fence.

Practice in Analysis

Decide on the analysis of each sentence, and then give the work orally in class.

1. The weary travellers landed at the airport in the early evening.
2. A pair of kingfishers darted across the bay.
3. A poor old man with a pack trudged along the road.
4. The ivy on the wall drooped over my window.
5. The doctor remained with the sick child during the night.
6. A cluster of burs clung to my sweater.
7. Many tall hollyhocks grow in our garden.
8. The sharp tinkle of little bells came from the sheepfold.
9. The lengthening rays of the rising sun stretched over the fields.
10. Scientific discoveries in agriculture added greatly to the country's wealth.
11. The ground between the hills sloped gradually to the river.
12. The hungry little fellow looked eagerly at the food.
13. A couple of neighbouring boys came to our house for matches.
14. The whistle of a train sounded in the distance.
15. The peaceful quiet of evening settled around us.

Write each sentence and analyse it graphically.

1. Dense clouds of smoke rose into the air.
2. The greatest discovery of all time came during the war.
3. Shouts of applause arose from every spectator.
4. The lonesome dog whined pitifully.
5. His route lay by the riverside.

6. A notice of the meeting appeared in every paper.
7. The cry of the hounds smote sharply on our ears.
8. A silvery full moon rode through the sky.
9. The driver pulled on the reins with all his might.
10. Heavy loads of lumber pass over the bridge daily.
11. The speed of the car shows on the speedometer.
12. The faithful dog watched for three days beside his master.
13. An open archway led into a spacious hall.
14. A large owl perched on a telephone pole.
15. Fossils of fish appear in many rocks.

Position of Modifiers

In the sentences you have studied, the subject with its modifiers has come first; then the predicate and predicate modifiers follow. However, the predicate may precede the subject, and often the predicate modifiers precede the predicate.

Example: (Through the small settlement) <u>sounded</u> [the] [wild] <u>cry</u> [of savage Indians.]

EXERCISE 14

Write each sentence and analyse it graphically. First get the subject and the predicate. Then decide where the modifiers belong.

1. At that very moment a mounted knight in armour approached swiftly.
2. Now fades the glimmering landscape from the sight.
3. For several years the men laboured earnestly together.
4. In the evenings May-flies danced over the water.
5. Beside the bed stood a rickety old chair.
6. Since the war many immigrants arrived in this country.
7. In the early days doctors in the country often travelled on horseback.
8. On several occasions disputes about the boundary line arose between the two countries.

9. From every window stared the faces of children.
10. By this time the hounds appeared in sight.
11. In every direction lofty mountains towered into the clouds.
12. During the war the national debt of Canada increased greatly.
13. In the fresh furrow walked a stealthy old crow.
14. At that time the price of copper rose steadily in every country.
15. In the early morning the victorious knight departed for his own castle.

EXERCISE 15

Analyse each sentence in writing.

1. For a whole week a jar of untouched olives sat on the pantry-shelf.
2. The close friendship of the boys lasted for several years.
3. With terrific speed the rocket flashed through the sky.
4. Snow on the highway interfered greatly with traffic.
5. For weeks the remnants of a defeated army wandered through the devastated land.
6. Through a tiny crack snow sifted into our cabin.
7. In many old castles repose relics of a glorious past.
8. Throughout the night a gentle rain pattered on the roof.
9. In these very fields our ancestors toiled hard.
10. At the circus wild animals paced about in their cages.
11. In former times ruddy flames roared up from many hearths.
12. At daybreak the schooner slipped into smoother water.
13. In the winter our supplies of food often diminished with alarming speed.
14. The names of all the players appeared in the paper.
15. In the spring birds of many kinds returned to the country-side.

Decide on the analysis of each sentence, and then give the work orally in class.

1. News of the heroic rescue spread quickly through the town.
2. After his speech the audience applauded enthusiastically.
3. In many eyes gleamed a sympathetic tear.
4. At this moment a queer little company of men emerged from the wood.
5. During the summer huge icebergs drift south into the Atlantic.
6. After school the boys often swam in the creek.
7. At length in our sheltered valley the winter suddenly began.
8. Across the field came the welcome caw of the first crow.
9. News of the atomic bomb spread rapidly throughout the world.
10. In a year the earth travels around the sun.
11. During the night smouldering embers kindled occasionally.
12. Through the dense forest a winding path led to the lake.
13. My dog always waits at the corner for me.
14. In parliament the young country lawyer advanced rapidly.
15. During the eclipse a dark shadow passed over the moon.

CHAPTER II

PARTS OF SPEECH

Parts of Speech, Relation of Words, Phrases

Nouns and Verbs

Turn to page 1, and read the sentences. Notice again that in the sentences given the word which names the person or thing spoken about is a NAME WORD, and the word which tells what is said about the person or thing is an ACTION WORD. Name words are called NOUNS, and action words are called VERBS.

EXERCISE 17

(a) Make a list of all the nouns in Exercises 2 and 3.
(b) Make a list of all the verbs in Exercises 2 and 3.
(c) Make a list of twenty name words, and a list of twenty action words.

Adjectives and Adverbs

For this lesson, turn to the sentences on page 2.
You have already learned:
(1) Each of these sentences contains a subject, a predicate, and a modifier.
(2) The subjects are name words or nouns, and the predicates are action words or verbs.
(3) The modifiers are of two kinds. Some modify subjects, and some modify predicates. This means that in these sentences some modify nouns, and some modify verbs.

Let us examine closely the modifiers of nouns and verbs in each of these sentences, and make a list of those

17

which modify nouns and a second list of those which modify verbs. For example:

The word *quickly* directs our thought to the verb *grows*. It is in the sentence to tell *how* grass *grows*.

The word *honest* carries our mind to the noun *men*. It makes us think of a quality in *men*.

In grammar, words which modify nouns are called ADJECTIVES, and words which modify verbs are called ADVERBS.

EXERCISE 18

(a) Make a list of all the adverbs in Exercises 2 and 3.
(b) Make a list of all the adjectives in Exercises 2 and 3.
(c) Classify all the words in Exercise 5 as nouns, verbs, adjectives, or adverbs.

Parts of Speech

When you classify words as you did in the last exercise, you give the PART OF SPEECH of each word. In other words, you give the grammatical value of each word in the sentence. There are eight parts of speech, and you have now learned to recognize four: noun, verb, adjective, and adverb.

Relation of Words

We say that one word in a sentence is related to another, because words work together to express thought. We are now ready to give the part of speech and the relation of a word to other words in the sentence.

Example: Good readers speak distinctly.

good — an adjective modifying the noun *readers*
readers — a noun, subject of the verb *speak*
speak — a verb having for its subject the noun *readers*
distinctly — an adverb modifying the verb *speak*

18

(a) Give in writing the part of speech and the relation of each word in Exercise 6.

(b) Give orally the part of speech and the relation of each word in Exercise 7.

Articles

The short modifiers *a, an, the,* are always classed as adjectives. They are the most frequent modifiers of nouns, and are called ARTICLES. *The* refers to some particular person or thing, and is called a DEFINITE ARTICLE. *A* and *an* do not refer to any particular person or thing, and are called INDEFINITE ARTICLES.

Example: The house at the corner burned.
　　　　　A 　house at the corner burned.

Pronouns

Examine the following pairs of sentences:

1. The boy went away.　　　3. The girl writes well.
　　He went away.　　　　　　　*She* writes well.
2. The men worked steadily.　4. The paper tears easily.
　　They worked steadily.　　　　*It* tears easily.

You see in the second sentence of each pair that a word is used instead of the noun in the first sentence. A word that is used instead of a noun is called a PRONOUN.

By substituting pronouns for nouns, we are able to speak and write without repeating the names of persons and things, which would take time and be tiresome.

Examples: Columbus landed here. $\left.{\text{*Columbus*} \atop \text{He}}\right\}$ discovered America.

The refrigerator leaks. $\left.{\text{*The refrigerator*} \atop \text{It}}\right\}$ should be repaired.

19

Select the pronouns in these sentences.

1. I come often.
2. This goes together easily.
3. She belongs here.
4. We arrived early.
5. It fits well.
6. Many entirely agreed.
7. That always hangs there.
8. He never came back.
9. Some try earnestly.
10. You never worked better.
11. Several stayed away to-day.
12. They moved in yester-day.

Give orally the part of speech and the relation of each word in the above sentences.

Phrases

Examine the following pairs of sentences:

1. *Large* trees grow *there.*
   Trees *of great size* grow *in that province.*
2. *Honourable* men live *everywhere.*
   Men *of honour* live *in every community.*
3. *Scientific* men investigate *carefully.*
   Men *of science* investigate *with care.*
4. *Desert* winds blow *strongly.*
   Winds *over the desert* blow *with great force.*
5. *Northern* rivers freeze *then.*
   Rivers *in the north* freeze *during the winter.*

Give the part of speech and the relation of each word in italics in the first sentence of each pair. Now analyse the second sentence of each pair.

From this work you see:

(1) Each adjective or adverb in italics in the first sentence of the pair is replaced by a word-group modifier in the second sentence.

(2) Each word-group has the same grammatical value as the single word it replaces.

(3) Each word-group is without subject and predicate.

A group of words which is used with the value of a single word, and which is without subject and predicate, is called a PHRASE.

A group of words with the value of an adjective is an ADJECTIVE PHRASE, and a group of words with the value of an adverb is an ADVERB PHRASE.

It is not always possible to replace the phrase in a sentence by a single word. For example, the phrases in the following sentences can not be replaced by single words:

What is the name *of this street?* (adjective phrase)
You did that *with my approval.* (adverb phrase)

However, in such cases you can readily decide whether the particular phrase has the value of an adjective or an adverb.

EXERCISE 22

(a) Give orally the kind and the relation of each phrase in Exercise 10.

(b) Write all the phrases in Exercise 11, and give the kind and the relation of each.

Example: We read in the library.

  in the library — an adverb phrase modifying the verb *read.*

EXERCISE 23

(a) State orally the kind and the relation of each phrase in Exercise 12.

(b) State orally the kind and the relation of each phrase in Exercise 13.

EXERCISE 24

(a) State orally the kind and the relation of each phrase in Exercise 14.

(b) State orally the kind and the relation of each phrase in Exercise 15.

Prepositions

Examine the words in italics in the following sentences:

The boys walked *to* the school.
The boys walked *from* the school.
The boys walked *through* the school.
The boys walked *around* the school.
The boys walked *past* the school.
The boys walked *into* the school.
The boys walked *in* the school.
The boys walked *towards* the school.

You notice that we can change completely the meaning of a sentence by changing only one word. Study the sentences again to see how an entirely different meaning is conveyed by each sentence through the change of the one word in italics. The new word expresses a different relationship between the verb *walked* and the noun *school*. If we substitute the pronoun *it* for the noun *school*, the change in relationship is then between the verb *walked* and the pronoun *it*.

A word which is placed before a noun or a pronoun to show its relation to another word is called a PRE-POSITION. It is always the first word in a phrase.

The use of a preposition should be given as follows:

Examples: Snow from the roof fell on the verandah.

   from — a preposition showing the relation between the noun *roof* and the noun *snow*.

   on — a preposition showing the relation between the noun *verandah* and the verb *fell*.

EXERCISE 25

Give in writing the use of each preposition in Exercise 11, and then give orally the use of each preposition in Exercises 12 and 13.

22

Other Adverbs

Examine the following pairs of sentences:

1. Better grain grows here.

2. Pleasant memories linger with me.
   Much better grain grows here.
   Very pleasant memories linger with me.

3. Hot days come in summer.
   Excessively hot days come in summer.

Give the part of speech and the relation of the first word in the first sentence of each pair.

Notice the relation of each word in italics in the second sentence of each pair. In every case this word modifies the adjective which follows it.

A word which modifies an adjective is an ADVERB.

Now examine the following sentences:

1. A deer runs fast.
   A deer runs *very* fast.

2. The guests arrived early.
   The guests arrived *too* early.

3. The students spoke well.
   The students spoke *exceedingly* well.

4. He went there.
   He went *nearly* there.

Give the part of speech and the relation of the last word in the first sentence of each pair.

Notice the relation of each word in italics in the second sentence of each pair. In every case this word modifies the adverb which follows it.

A word which modifies an adverb is also an ADVERB.

We can now give the definition of an adverb. An ADVERB is a word that modifies a verb, an adjective, or another adverb.

Give in writing the relation of each adverb.

1. The road climbs very steeply.
2. He spoke quite freely about his experiences.
3. Scarcely enough food remained in the fort.
4. An exceedingly old man lives there.
5. People moved away hurriedly.
6. They worked with slightly different methods.
7. Some animals barely exist during the winter.
8. An entirely new machine works well.
9. Only honest men work here.
10. The prisoners nearly escaped.
11. The train travels too slowly.
12. We arrived here just now.
13. Much hotter days come in July.
14. I merely glanced at the picture.
15. Very small trees often grow quite thickly.

Give orally the relation of each adverb.

1. The pilot steered straight ahead.
2. Two kittens frisked playfully over the lawn.
3. That happens quite frequently.
4. The plane climbed nearly perpendicularly.
5. Almost perfect weather lasted throughout the summer.
6. The screech of the siren drew steadily nearer.
7. Your dog growls rather viciously.
8. The Scandinavians protect their forests carefully from fire.
9. Immediately the boat turned about.
10. A very dark cloud hung directly overhead.
11. The last swimmer lagged far behind.
12. Most naturalists observe closely.
13. An unusually severe storm swept over the city.
14. The owl blinked continually.

Conjunctions

Examine the following sentences:

Boys *and* girls play in the yard.
The men shouted *and* sang in the street.
A long *but* mild winter passed pleasantly.
Slowly *and* sadly the people walked along.
Sheep graze in the valleys *and* on the hills.

By examining the words in italics we see:
(1) In the first sentence two nouns which are the subject of the verb *play* are joined by *and*. This is called a COMPOUND SUBJECT.
(2) In the second sentence two verbs which have the subject *men* are joined by *and*. This is called a COMPOUND PREDICATE.
(3) In the third sentence two adjectives which modify the same noun are joined by *but*.
(4) In the fourth sentence two adverbs which modify the same verb are joined by *and*.
(5) In the fifth sentence two adverb phrases which modify the same verb are joined by *and*.

Notice that in each sentence the joined words or phrases are used in the same way; that is, they have the same relation in the sentence. A word which joins words or phrases used in the same way in a sentence is called a CONJUNCTION.

The use of a conjunction should be given as follows:

Examples: Horses *or* cows pasture in that field every summer.
People live in houses of brick *and* of stone.

   or — a conjunction joining the nouns *horses* and *cows*, which form the compound subject of the verb *pasture*.
   and — a conjunction joining the two adjective phrases *of brick* and *of stone*, which modify the noun *houses*.

25

Give in writing the use of each conjunction, and the relation of the joined parts.

1. The teacher spoke firmly but kindly.
2. We went and returned by the same route.
3. Smoke escaped through the windows and through the doors.
4. The travellers on the train slept or read.
5. Weary but determined soldiers marched to battle.
6. A long and heavy canoe passed slowly.
7. Eclipses of the sun and of the moon occur at certain times.
8. Poor but honest people live here.
9. I gazed into the sky and over the ocean.
10. Men from the navy and from the army marched together.
11. Friends and foes mingled in a vast throng.
12. Wood or coal burns well in this furnace.

Give orally the use of each conjunction, and the relation of the joined parts.

1. The Indians hunted and fished for food.
2. Swiftly and fiercely the flames leaped forward.
3. We always camp by a lake or beside a river.
4. Parcels of equipment and of supplies lay everywhere on the wharf.
5. Rare and expensive paintings hung on the walls.
6. He pitches or catches equally well.
7. The early settlers sowed and mowed by hand.
8. Slowly but surely the damaged ship crawled into port.
9. I study in the morning and in the evening.
10. We ate and slept in the same tent.
11. A small but courageous dog lay at his master's feet.
12. Men and women bowl in this alley.
13. We went and returned by the same route.
14. He speaks quickly but distinctly.

CHAPTER III

VERBS AND COMPLETIONS

Objects of Verbs, Transitive and Intransitive Verbs,
Copula Verbs, Subjective Completions, Verb Phrases

Objects of Verbs

Study the following sentences carefully:

The horses pulled the *load.*
The mouse ate the *cheese.*
The hunter shot a *deer.*
The girl broke the *dish.*
The policeman raised his *hand.*
The dog bit *him.*

Try to analyse each sentence. In each italicized word you see something new. You discover a noun or pronoun which is not the subject of a verb, and which is not part of a phrase.

By examining the sentences, you see that each verb is an ACTION WORD, and that the noun or pronoun following it names the RECEIVER OF THE ACTION. In other words, it names the person or thing the action is directed towards.

A word which names the receiver of the verb's action is called an OBJECT OF THE VERB.

The relation of an object should be given as follows:

Examples: The boy closed the *door.*
　　　　　We saw *them.*
door — a noun, object of the verb *closed.*
them — a pronoun, object of the verb *saw.*

27

Give in writing the relation of each object.

1. The girls painted the floor.
2. The boys shovel the snow.
3. We ate our lunch at noon.
4. You passed them on the road.
5. Carpenters build houses.
6. I gave it to the man.
7. She knows the song well.
8. The ship crossed the ocean in six days.
9. They carried him upstairs.
10. We borrow books from the library.
11. The nurse placed the flowers in a bowl.
12. The children picked the berries.
13. She paints pictures in her spare time.
14. Alan caught a mink in his muskrat trap.

Analysis of Sentences with Objects

In the graphic analysis of a sentence which has an object, we place three lines under the object. A curved line indicates a modifier of the object.

Example: [The] Romans built good roads (in Britain).

In the written analysis of a sentence, the object and its modifiers are usually placed last.

Example: Skilful packers place the delicious apples in boxes.
  Bare Subject — packers
  Modifier of the Bare Subject — skilful
  Bare Predicate — place
  Modifier of the Bare Predicate — in boxes
  Object — apples
  Modifiers of the Object — (1) the (2) delicious

Write each sentence and analyse it graphically.

1. We gathered dry sticks for our fire.
2. The boys carried the wood into the shed.
3. She hung her coat on a hook.
4. The grocer placed the cans on a shelf.
5. Squirrels gather nuts for winter food.
6. The boy made a good raft.
7. Birds eat the seeds of many fruits.
8. The men crossed the river in a boat.
9. He drove the cows to the pasture.
10. Many farmers plough their fields in the fall.
11. The boy caught a large fish.
12. They moved the machine to another farm.
13. The engine belched clouds of smoke.
14. The boys sharpened their skates for the game.

Analyse each sentence in writing.

1. The new equipment soon cleared the snow from the streets.
2. The boys made a skating rink near the school.
3. Then the dog led the hunters to his wounded master.
4. We always raise the flag on public holidays.
5. He helped the blind man across the street.
6. We scored a goal in the last quarter.
7. The early explorers made many important discoveries.
8. Sometimes a policeman directs traffic at the busy corners.
9. Musicians tune their instruments carefully.
10. They heard the throb of the engine plainly.
11. Later the crippled destroyer rejoined the other ships.
12. The pupils of rural schools often plant trees in the yard.
13. We raised every window in the room.
14. The farmer built a fence around his orchard.

Decide on the analysis of each sentence, and then give the work orally in class.

1. At last the searchers found the child beside an old barn.
2. The servants placed the best food before him.
3. Tightly he held the precious toy in his hand.
4. The old gentleman has a hearty laugh.
5. Often from the lonely lake he heard the cry of a loon.
6. After this great victory he led his soldiers to the city.
7. Then Columbus made a new settlement on the island.
8. The constant drip of water wears holes in stones.
9. The modest wants of every day
   The toil of every day supplied.
10. Through much effort men discover the secrets of nature.
11. Some careless folk the deed forgot.
12. At evening I heard the loud call of the whip-poor-will.
13. Several of the contestants answered all the questions correctly.
14. Then from a rusted iron hook,
    A bunch of ponderous keys he took.

Differences in Action Verbs

Sometimes the action of the verb is not physical, that is, it cannot be readily seen or perceived. Nevertheless the verb does express an action which might be considered mental or hidden in some way.

Study the following sentences, and notice that each sentence contains an object, but in the second sentence of each pair the verb does not show a physical action.

1. He *lifted* his hat.   2. The boy *wiped* his shoes.
   My father *owns* a car.   He *considered* my offer at once.
3. He *threw* the ball.
   Our garden *supplies* vegetables for several families.

Study the verbs of these sentences to see whether the action is direct or hidden. Then analyse each sentence orally.

1. Farmers spend much time in the fields.
2. Some subjects require careful study.
3. Fire-escapes on schools ensure the safety of pupils.
4. The setting sun announces the close of day.
5. Trappers in Arctic regions endure many hardships.
6. In our conversation we recalled the names of many friends.
7. In pioneer days an exciting adventure befell a young trapper.
8. At closing time the janitor locks the door.
9. Such businesses usually pay handsome dividends.
10. The majority of people distinctly remember their early school days.

Transitive and Intransitive Verbs

Examine the following pairs of sentences:

1. The boys *rolled* the lawn. Waves *rolled* toward the shore.

2. The pupils *write* letters. The pupils *write* well.

3. They *grow* vegetables. Weeds *grow* rapidly.

4. Boys *fly* kites. Birds *fly* fast.

5. We *passed* many houses. The days *passed* slowly.

Analyse each of the above sentences orally. Notice particularly:

(1) In every sentence the verb shows action.

(2) In the first sentence of each pair the verb is followed by an object. This object is required to complete the meaning of the sentence.

(3) In the second sentence of each pair the same verb is not followed by an object.

31

When the verb takes an object, we say that it is a TRANSITIVE VERB. Transitive means *to go across*. The action in the verb goes across to the object. When the verb does not take an object, we say that it is an INTRANSITIVE VERB. Intransitive means *not transitive*.

The use of the verb in the sentence tells us whether it is transitive or intransitive. The same word may be a transitive verb in one sentence, and an intransitive verb in another. Notice this again from these examples.

Examples: The man *moves* furniture. The man *moves* quickly.
He *works* his horses hard. He *works* in a store.

EXERCISE 35

(a) Classify the verbs as transitive or intransitive.

1. The storm raged during the whole night.
2. The bears ate the food in our tent.
3. The early settlers fenced their fields.
4. The students listened attentively.
5. The apples fell from the tree.
6. He guided the trembling child along.
7. They built a new school.
8. The policemen came quickly.
9. He refused the offer of a handsome gift.
10. We walked through the garden.
11. Kings live in palaces.
12. The boys moved the seats.
13. All the pupils listened intently.
14. The shepherds watched their flocks.

(b) Write sentences using each word as a transitive verb and as an intransitive verb:

ride, climb, see, study, play, bend, build, write, stand, assist, teach, plough, shake, sound, eat.

Copula Verbs

Study the following sentences, noticing the verbs, and the words in italics that follow them:

1. The boy is *ambitious*.
2. I am *happy*.
3. The day was *hot*.
4. The questions are *easy*.
5. The girls were *friends*.
6. The melons seem *ripe*.
7. He became a *doctor*.
8. The road looks *muddy*.
9. The chocolates taste *delicious*.

An examination of the sentences shows:

(1) Some of the words in italics are adjectives which describe or modify the subject.

(2) Some of the words in italics are nouns and stand for the same person or thing as the subject.

(3) In every sentence the verb needs the word in italics to help complete the meaning. Prove this by reading the sentences, leaving off the words which follow the verbs.

(4) The verbs in the sentences above do not express action, but are used to *link* or *join* or *couple* the completing word to the subject.

Verbs which link or join or couple the completing word to the subject are called COPULA VERBS.

Copula verbs are comparatively few in number. The most common are: *am, is, are, was, were, seem, become, appear, look, feel, taste, sound, smell, grow, turn.*

It is interesting to notice that a few words can be used as transitive, intransitive, and copula verbs.

Examples: He *turned* the wheel. He *turned* quickly. He *turned* pale.

Boys *grow* potatoes. Boys *grow* fast. Boys *grow* sleepy.

It is also well to note that the verbs *am, is, are, was,* and *were* are often intransitive.

Examples: He *is* here. They *were* in the yard.

Subjective Completion

Let us examine again the words which complete the predicate in the sentences you have just studied. We have found that some are nouns, and stand for the same person or thing as the subject. Others are adjectives which modify the subject. These words help the copula verb to form the complete predicate. A word which helps a copula verb to form the complete predicate is called a SUBJECTIVE COMPLETION.

When a subjective completion is an adjective, it is called a PREDICATE ADJECTIVE; when it is a noun, it is CALLED a PREDICATE NOUN.

The relation of a subjective completion should be given as follows:

Examples: The man feels *weary.*

The men are *partners.*

weary — a predicate adjective completing the copula verb *feels* and modifying the noun *man.*

partners — a predicate noun completing the copula verb *are* and standing for *men.*

EXERCISE 36

Give in writing the relation of each subjective completion.

1. The river was swift.
2. These men are good swimmers.
3. Our canoe is red.
4. The pie tastes delicious.
5. That pupil is a fast reader.
6. The child was peevish.
7. My pet squirrel became a nuisance.
8. This apple seems ripe.
9. The brothers are lawyers.
10. His home is his castle.

Give orally the relation of each subjective completion.

1. The dog is a wolfhound.
2. That parrot was my pet.
3. A tomato is a fruit.
4. Potatoes are tubers.
5. Her son became king.
6. Kittens are playful.
7. The berries look ripe.
8. Violets smell sweet.
9. Jays are inquisitive.
10. The king grew old.
11. The bathers were cold.
12. The water felt warm.
13. Your chum looks thin.
14. The children were noisy.
15. The bear became angry.
16. The voices sound loud.
17. This milk tastes sour.
18. The man turned pale.
19. Olives seem salty.
20. Monkeys appear clever.

Verb Phrases

Study the following sentences, noticing especially the words in italics:

1. The pupils *sing*.
   The pupils *are singing*.
   The pupils *have sung*.
   The pupils *have been singing*.

2. He *reads* well.
   He *was reading* well.
   He *had read* well.
   He *had been reading* well.

3. I *write* on the board.
   I *shall write* on the board.
   I *shall be writing* on the board.
   I *shall have written* on the board.

In the first sentence of each group, the verb is only one word. In the other sentences of each group, the verb consists of two or more words. A verb which consists of two or more words is called a VERB PHRASE.

The word in a verb phrase which expresses the main idea is called the PRINCIPAL VERB. The first sentence of each group shows the principal verb. Notice that the

35

principal verb has different forms. The additional or helping words are called AUXILIARY VERBS. They are used mainly to show a change of time.

Do not confuse verb phrases with prepositional phrases. A verb phrase is simply a verb consisting of more than one word. It is proper to refer to a verb phrase as the verb or bare predicate of the sentence.

EXERCISE 38

Name the principal and auxiliary verbs in each verb phrase.

1. I have eaten my dinner.
2. We shall go there tomorrow.
3. He was lying on the ground.
4. They were running in the yard.
5. The pupils have been sliding on the frozen pond.
6. He had said that before.
7. The boy is reading a good book.
8. Our friends are coming now.
9. The doctor did visit the sick man.
10. The birds have been flying south lately.
11. The men will hunt for deer.
12. We shall be living there soon.
13. I have never seen the ocean.
14. She was visiting in the country.
15. The policemen had been wearing new uniforms.

CHAPTER IV

KINDS OF SENTENCES

Kinds of Sentences, Complete Analysis, Objects of Prepositions

Kinds of Sentences

Study the following sentences. Notice how each pair differs from the other pairs.

1. They left for town early.
   The boys play ball in the yard.

2. Where are you going?
   Who has my hat?

3. Play more quietly.
   Do write often.

The sentences in the first pair make a statement or assert something. These are called ASSERTIVE SENTENCES. All the sentences you have studied so far in exercises have been assertive sentences.

In the second pair, the sentences ask questions. These are called INTERROGATIVE SENTENCES. In writing, an interrogative sentence is followed by a question mark, which is also called an interrogation mark.

In the third pair, both sentences give commands, but the second command is softened, and might be considered a request. These are called IMPERATIVE SENTENCES.

Interjections

Words used to express strong feeling, such as surprise, excitement, despair, and anger, are called INTERJECTIONS.

Examples:

Oh, I did not notice you.
Hurrah! We won the game.
Hark! Someone is coming.
Hush! Do not disturb her.
Ah! That sounds better.
Hello! When did you come?

If the interjection is an emphatic or forceful expression, it is followed by an exclamation mark, as in the last five examples. If it does not appear forceful, it is followed by a comma, as in the first sentence. In the analysis of sentences, interjections are omitted.

Exclamatory Sentences

A whole sentence is sometimes used to give expression to a strong feeling. This is called an EXCLAMATORY SENTENCE. It always ends with an exclamation mark.

Examples: How glad I am to see you!
What a perfect day this is!
What beautiful roses you have!

An exclamatory sentence often begins with an interjection.

Examples: Oh, forget about it!
Well, I am glad that examination is over!
Indeed, that is good news!

38

Analysis of Imperative, Interrogative, and Exclamatory Sentences

Notice that the subject of an imperative sentence is omitted, and that it must be supplied when we analyse the sentence.

Examples: Sit in the front seat. *You* sit (in the front seat).

Take your bicycle from the porch.

You take your bicycle (from the porch).

In the analysis of an interrogative sentence, re-arrange the sentence mentally to place the subject and predicate at the beginning. Then analyse the sentence as it is given.

Examples: (When) is he going (away)? What do you see?

(He is going away when?)   *(You do see what?)*

In the analysis of an exclamatory sentence, re-arrange the sentence mentally, to place the subject and predicate at the beginning, and analyse it as it is given.

Examples: (How well) he spoke! What a mistake he made!

(He spoke how well!)   *(He made what a mistake!)*

EXERCISE 39

Analyse each sentence in writing.

1. Did you find your pen?
2. Come with me to the circus.
3. What did you have for dinner?
4. Call for me in the morning.
5. What huge pumpkins you have!
6. Leave the letter on the table.
7. Have you bought a ticket for the concert?
8. Arrange the flowers neatly in the dish.
9. Which road do we take?
10. Sorry, I do not know the answer.

There and Not

The words *there* and *not* require special study.

You have been accustomed to using the word *there* as an adverb, meaning *in that place*, or *to that place*. Sometimes, however, the word *there* is used as an introductory word which fills out the sentence to give it smoothness. When the word *there* is used in this way, it is called an EXPLETIVE. It gets its name from a Latin word which means *to fill out*. We omit expletives when analysing sentences because they are not related grammatically to other words in the sentence.

Examples: He went *there* (adverb).
　　　　　There is no answer (expletive).

Study the following sentences, and note the use of the word *there* in each one:

There may be a storm soon.
They went *there* for the holiday.
Then *there* came a heavy frost.
There was a knock at the door.
There is nothing *there*.

The word *not* is an adverb. It may modify a verb, an adjective, or another adverb.

Study the use of the word *not* in each of the following sentences:

He is *not* at home (adverb modifying the verb *is*).
Not sufficient warning was given (adverb modifying the adjective *sufficient*).
Not nearly sufficient warning was given (adverb modifying the adverb *nearly*).
Do *not* answer in that manner (adverb modifying the verb *do answer*).
Medicine will *not* cure him (adverb modifying the verb *will cure*).

Note that when a word modifies a modifier (of the bare subject, bare predicate, or object), the two words are placed together in analysis to make a single modifier.

Examples: [The] [extremely bright] lights dazzled the eyes of the driver.

I shall see you (again) (very soon).

There is [too much] noise (in the room).
(We omit the expletive.)

EXERCISE 40

(a) Write each sentence and analyse it graphically.

(b) Explain orally in class the uses of the words *there* and *not*.

1. There is not enough coal in the stove.
2. Not vainly did the pilgrims seek new homes.
3. There are strong lights in this room.
4. She will not see you tomorrow.
5. Not many days are left for shopping.
6. There was lightning in the night.
7. I have not forgotten your kindness.
8. There is room for your hats on the rack.
9. They did not go to the meeting.
10. He has not yet arrived.
11. There is a letter for you there.
12. There are thirty days in September.
13. There were many exhibits at the flower show.
14. I did not see you there.
15. There are some thrilling stories in that book.
16. There were not many parents there.
17. There is time for another game.

Complete Detailed Analysis

You have learned all the parts of a sentence, and have now reached the last step in the kind of analysis that we have been doing. We call this DETAILED ANALYSIS. In detailed graphic analysis use a wavy line to show a subjective completion and a curved line to show a modifier of a subjective completion.

Examples of Graphic Analysis:

(At once) [the] [little] girl became a beautiful gold statue.

[The] child seems very sick.

[The] wood is not sufficiently dry.

Example of Written Analysis:

At once the little girl became a beautiful gold statue.
Bare Subject — girl
Modifiers of the Bare Subject — (1) the (2) little
Bare Predicate — became
Modifier of the Bare Predicate — at once
Subjective Completion — statue
Modifiers of the Subjective Completion — (1) a (2) beautiful (3) gold

EXERCISE 41

Write each sentence and analyse it graphically.

1. The life of a lion-hunter was dangerous.
2. Plans for the hike are now ready.
3. On the trip the plane flew over dense forests.
4. Good highways connect all the principal towns of the province.
5. In the lock they saw several freighters.
6. The lake looks beautiful at sunrise.
7. Were the houses of the settlers cold in winter?
8. The roar of the engines faded in the distance.
9. A sudden storm turned the ship from its regular course.

Write each sentence and analyse it graphically.

1. A new boy came to our school today.
2. Previously we needed a player on our team.
3. The native was a devoted servant of the explorer.
4. In a terrific storm the plucky little ship nosed her way into port.
5. Put the new tire in the truck.
6. I do not know any boys on the other team.
7. Meat was scarce during that long winter.
8. The mining engineer was having great difficulty with sliding rock.
9. The sky above us was inky black.
10. All the air a solemn stillness holds.
11. Why were you climbing the fence?
12. For several years we had not planted a garden.

Decide on the analysis of each sentence, and then give the work orally in class.

1. In the spring our boys play baseball in vacant lots.
2. Between the hunter and the deer was a wide swamp.
3. I have read several stories about tigers.
4. We have been living here for a long time.
5. The dwellings of the natives were very small.
6. Then the fireman moved very cautiously along the ledge.
7. On every occasion his good manners were noticeable.
8. We have heard your words of warning.
9. Canada is fortunately a country of great natural resources.
10. Since those early days life on Canadian farms has become happier and easier.
11. In the autumn the leaves of the maples are very colourful.
12. On long walking trips Scott gathered material for his novels.

Connected Phrases

In some sentences several phrases are connected, with one phrase modifying a word in another phrase. In such cases, the two or more separate phrases make one modifier for purposes of sentence analysis.

Example: Rain poured *through the roof of our cabin in the pines.*

The modifier of the predicate is *through the roof of our cabin in the pines.*

Taken as three separate phrases, we show the relation of these phrases as follows:

through the roof — adverb phrase modifying the verb *poured.*
of our cabin — adjective phrase modifying the noun *roof.*
in the pines — adjective phrase modifying the noun *cabin.*

EXERCISE 44

Decide on the analysis of each sentence, and then give the work orally in class.

1. The birds ate the crumbs from our table.
2. We read by the light of the candle.
3. The antics of a clown in rags amused the children.
4. At this time of the year fishermen mend their nets.
5. In June an eagle built a nest in a tall pine about a mile from our cottage.
6. He came up over the hill in the flush of the early dawn.
7. On the day in question they had fastened their rope to a tree on the top of the cliff.
8. Presently the vacant space at the window was filled by another form.
9. In front of us a huge flock of sheep filed slowly down that narrow trail in the mountains.
10. There in the midst of its farms reposed the Acadian village.

Objects of Prepositions

You learned that a preposition is the first word in a phrase. The last word in a phrase is called the OBJECT OF THE PREPOSITION. Sometimes the words of a phrase are separated, as in the second example below.

We give the relation of the object of a preposition as follows:

Examples: The petals dropped off the *rose.*

Whom are you writing to?

rose — a noun, object of the preposition *off.*
whom — a pronoun, object of the preposition *to.*

EXERCISE 45

Select the object of each preposition and give its relation in writing.

1. The river is deep at that spot.
2. Whom did you get it from?
3. Offers of help came from several friends.
4. Will you take me with you?
5. I shall call at your house for the parcel on my way to school.
6. What were you pointing at?
7. Many tons of coal for winter use were stored in the cellar during the summer.
8. I read about it in the paper.
9. Whom were you talking to?
10. We waited at the corner for her.
11. Hearty applause came from every part of the room.
12. Through a hole in the dyke water poured over the land.
13. The sailor pointed toward the island.
14. During the summer vacation I sleep in a tent.

Different Uses of the Same Word

The use of a word in the sentence determines what part of speech it is. In the following sentences study the words in italics, which show this clearly:

1. We need your *help*. (noun)
   We *help* our parents. (verb)

2. The *iron* is hot. (noun)
   It is an *iron* rod. (adjective)
   They *iron* clothes. (verb)

3. I have been here *before*. (adverb)
   He sat *before* the fireplace. (preposition)

4. Some men work *hard*. (adverb)
   That is a *hard* task. (adjective)

5. Our soldiers defend the *right*. (noun)
   Judges often *right* injustices. (verb)
   That is the *right* answer. (adjective)
   He always acts *right*. (adverb)

EXERCISE 46

(a) Compose sentences using each of the following words as a noun. Then compose sentences using each word as a verb:

hope, mention, hurt, permit, review

(b) Compose sentences using each of the following words as a preposition and an adverb:

under, by, over, through, without

(c) Compose sentences using each of the following words as an adverb and an adjective:

well, daily, fast, high, deep

(d) Compose sentences using each of the following words as a noun, verb, and adjective:

wrong, telephone, paper, return, blind

CHAPTER V

REVIEW

REVIEW—Adverbs

EXERCISE 47

(a) Review carefully the work on adverbs on pages 23 and 24.

(b) Give orally the relation of each adverb in Exercise 26.

REVIEW—Adjectives

EXERCISE 48

Give orally the relation of each adjective in Exercise 42.

REVIEW—Phrases

EXERCISE 49

(a) Study again the work on phrases on pages 20 and 21.

(b) Pick out the phrases from the sentences in Exercises 43 and 44. Then in class, give orally the kind and the relation of each phrase.

REVIEW—Objects of Verbs

EXERCISE 50

(a) Study again the work on objects of verbs on pages 27 and 28.

(b) Give orally the relation of each object of a verb in Exercises 30 and 31.

REVIEW—Subjective Completion
(a) Review the work on copula verbs and subjective completions on pages 33 and 34.

(b) Give orally the relation of each subjective completion in Exercises 36 and 41.

REVIEW—Conjunctions
EXERCISE 52
(a) Study carefully the work on conjunctions on page 25.

(b) Give orally the answers to Exercise 28.

EXERCISE 53
(a) Write two sentences with a conjunction joining two words which form a compound subject.

(b) Write two sentences with a conjunction joining two words which form a compound object.

(c) Write two sentences with a conjunction joining two verbs which form a compound predicate.

(d) Write two sentences with a conjunction joining two adjectives.

(e) Write two sentences with a conjunction joining two adverbs.

(f) Write two sentences with a conjunction joining two adjective phrases.

(g) Write two sentences with a conjunction joining two adverb phrases.

REVIEW—General
EXERCISE 54
(a) Write five sentences with a verb phrase forming the predicate of each sentence.

(b) Write five sentences with an adverb modifying a verb.

(c) Write five sentences with an adverb modifying an adjective.

48

(d) Write five sentences with an adverb modifying an adverb.

(e) Write three sentences with two adjectives and two adverbs in each.

(a) Write three short interrogative sentences and analyse each graphically.

(b) Write three imperative sentences and analyse each graphically.

(c) Write three exclamatory sentences and analyse each graphically.

(d) Write three sentences with an adverb phrase at the beginning of each.

(e) Write three sentences with an adverb phrase at the end of each.

(f) Write three sentences with an adverb phrase and an adjective phrase in each.

(a) Write sentences using each of the following groups of words as an adverb phrase, and then as an adjective phrase:

on the ground; in the boat; over the ocean;
by the building; for your help; through the forest

(b) Write five sentences in which the verbs have objects.

(c) Write five sentences in which the verbs are followed by subjective completions.

REVIEW—Relation of Words
Give in writing the part of speech, and the relation or the use of each word.

1. The wood of this tree is very strong and hard.
2. Presently the owner of the cabin appeared in the doorway.
3. The giant plane flew swiftly over land and sea.
4. They had concealed their discovery for two years.

Study these paragraphs and decide on the part of speech and the relation or the use of each word. Then give the work orally in class.

The sky was friendly. We recognized some of the stars. The Great Dipper was there. The North Star was also there. The studded belt of Orion was bright. The Little Dipper was faint but clear. Other stars winked and sparkled at us from the sky. The snow winked and sparkled at us from the ground. It was a diamond-studded night. White beauty was everywhere.

We circled the silent islands with their empty cabins. Then we turned for home. The moon was aloft now. She had grown prouder and colder. The stars were colder too. The air was still. From the hill came the bark of a dog. It came again and again. It and the crunch of our snow-shoes were the only noises of the night.

Adapted from "White Beauty" by Charles B. Pyper.

REVIEW—Detailed Analysis

Analyse each sentence in writing.

1. For hours huge waves lashed the shore of the tiny island.
2. Where did you get this exciting book?
3. From our seat in the gallery we could hear every word of the play.
4. In dusky pods the milkweed
   Its hidden silk has spun.
5. Many farmers in Canada are now harvesting their grain with combines.
6. My golden spurs now bring to me.

7. The weary hunter kindled a fire on the bank of the river.
8. We piled with care our nightly stack
   Of wood against the chimney-back.
9. The black panther is a ferocious beast.
10. Oft did the harvest to our sickle yield.
11. There are still many undiscovered lakes in Canada.
12. The ranger reported the forest fire from his tower on the hill.

Study each sentence to decide on its analysis, and then give the work orally in class.

1. Those red candles on the table are very pretty.
2. Slowly the huge grizzly lumbered down the mountain-side.
3. Then a whirling flake of snow fell gently on the old man's hand.
4. For many people in a city the parks provide enjoyment in summer.
5. The golden sea its mirror spreads
   Beneath the golden sky.
6. At dawn the ship found herself in the thick of the fight.
7. The greatest events in the world's history have occurred in this century.
8. The blazing logs in the fireplace furnished ample light during the winter evening.
9. From the mill the early settlers often carried sacks of flour on their backs to their homes.
10. We dropped the seed o'er hill and plain
    Beneath the sun of May.
11. In front of our house we planted a row of maples.
12. Through vales of grass and meads of flowers
    Our ploughs their furrows made.

CHAPTER VI

NOUNS AND PRONOUNS

Common and Proper Nouns

Examine the following sentences and notice the difference in the italicized nouns in each pair:

1. They built a *city* there.
   They built *Victoria* there.

2. The *explorer* sailed along the coast.
   Cook sailed along the coast.

3. A *nurse* became famous.
   Florence Nightingale became famous.

4. The *country* has vast resources.
   Canada has vast resources.

5. The *river* flows into the ocean.
   The *St. Lawrence* flows into the ocean.

The noun *city* in the first sentence might refer to *any* city anywhere in the world. The noun in the second sentence of this pair names one particular city, *Victoria*. In the same way, the noun *explorer* might be *any* explorer, but the noun *Cook* names one particular man, *Captain Cook*.

A noun which applies to any one of a class of things is called a COMMON NOUN. A noun which names one particular person, place, or thing is called a PROPER NOUN. Notice that the name of one particular person, place, or thing is always shown with a capital letter.

(a) Classify the nouns as common or proper.

1. The town of Whitby is close to Toronto.
2. The city has a library on King Street. It was endowed by Andrew Carnegie.
3. Easter and Christmas are special days.
4. The shortest month is February.
5. Sunday is the first day of the week.
6. Cuba and Iceland are islands.
7. We crossed the ocean on the Queen Mary.
8. David Livingstone discovered and named the Victoria Falls in Africa.
9. Shakespeare wrote many famous plays and poems.
10. Montreal is the largest city in Canada.
11. Bunyan wrote *Pilgrim's Progress* in prison.
12. Queen Victoria was greatly loved by her people.
13. Mexico is on the southern border of the United States of America.

(b) Give a proper noun to correspond with each common noun in the following list, and give a common noun to correspond with each proper noun:

Examples: lake — Ontario; Edison — inventor.

lake	girl	Hudson	gulf
river	day	newspaper	Vesuvius
island	Paris	ship	railway
isthmus	Florida	king	ocean
strait	month	Tuesday	street
Edison	province	country	Tennyson
Panama	Caribbean	woman	Robin Hood

Study of Pronouns

Pronouns are classified in certain ways because they differ in nature.

(a) Study the sentences which follow and decide on the analysis of each sentence.

(b) Make a list of all the pronouns in the sentences, noticing similarities and differences.

1. I have seen that before.
2. He hurt himself.
3. We met her there.
4. Are you going with me?
5. I did not see you
6. It is your book.
7. This is my pen.
8. Whom did you want?
9. Which did you choose?
10. We went with them.
11. Another will take my place.
12. All have listened attentively.
13. Some will believe anything.
14. Everybody felt sorry for her.
15. Something hit him on the head.
16. He always considered the welfare of others.
17. One should not say that.
18. This is a valuable picture.
19. Several applied for the position.
20. Each should bring a notebook.
21. You are keeping him from his work.
22. Anyone may make a mistake.
23. Few knew about their trouble.
24. Many went to the meeting.
25. What did he say about it?
26. Who gave the money to him?

Classes of Pronouns

Pronouns which stand for persons are called PERSONAL PRONOUNS. The following are personal pronouns:

I, me, he, him, you, we, us, they, them, she, hers, his, yours, theirs, mine

Pronouns which are used in asking questions are called INTERROGATIVE PRONOUNS. The following are interrogative pronouns:

who, whom, whose, which, what

Pronouns which point out a particular person or thing are called DEMONSTRATIVE PRONOUNS. They get this name from the Latin word, *demonstro*, which means *point out*. The following are demonstrative pronouns:

this, that, these, those

Example: The books are on the table. *These* are mine, but *those* belong to Tom.

Pronouns which stand for no particular person or thing are called INDEFINITE PRONOUNS. The following are indefinite pronouns:

some, few, any, all, several, one, none, both, either, neither, many, each, others

Also compounds of the above, as:

someone, somebody, something, anyone, anybody, anything, everyone, everybody, everything, no one

EXERCISE 63

Classify the pronouns in Exercise 62 as personal, interrogative, demonstrative, or indefinite.

Pronominal Adjectives

Give the part of speech and the relation of each word in italics.

1. *This* book belongs to me.
2. *That* book belongs to you.
3. *Which* way did they go?
4. *Whose* son are you?
5. *My* work is easy.
6. *Some* men are fortunate.

Your study of the italicized words in the above sentences shows:

(1) These words are adjectives, since they modify nouns.
(2) They are pronouns, since they stand for persons or things.

Words which have the value of both pronouns and adjectives are called PRONOMINAL ADJECTIVES.

The relation of a pronominal adjective should be given as follows:

Examples: These are *your* gloves. *Which* pair do you want?

your — a pronominal adjective modifying the noun *gloves*.

which — a pronominal adjective modifying the noun *pair*.

EXERCISE 64

Select the pronominal adjectives and give the relation of each.

1. May I have your ruler?
2. Her writing is good.
3. We need their help.
4. They liked its colour.
5. Our time is precious.
6. These days are short.
7. Any seat will suit me.
8. That roast looks tender.
9. Which hat did you buy?
10. That building is very old.
11. Whose pencil are you using?
12. Some boys are skilful carpenters.
13. Several members were late.
14. My brother plays hockey well.

Person in Pronouns

There are three kinds of PERSONAL PRONOUNS, as follows:

(1) I, me, mine; we, us, ours
(2) You, yours; thou, thee, thine, ye
   (*Thou, thee, thine,* and *ye* are not commonly used)
(3) he, him, his; she, her, hers; it, its; they, them, theirs

A study of these lists shows:

(1) The pronouns in the first list stand for the person or persons speaking. These are called pronouns of the FIRST PERSON.

(2) The pronouns in the second list stand for the person or persons spoken to. These are called pronouns of the SECOND PERSON.

(3) The pronouns in the third list stand for the person or persons spoken about. These are called pronouns of the THIRD PERSON.

Pronouns such as *myself, himself, yourself, herself, itself, ourselves, yourselves, themselves,* are called COMPOUND PERSONAL PRONOUNS.

It should be noted that interrogative, demonstrative, and indefinite pronouns stand for the person or thing spoken about, and are of the third person. All nouns are of the third person.

Number in Nouns and Pronouns

Nouns and pronouns usually change their form to show whether one or more than one is meant.

Examples:

(one):	I	me	he	girl	sheaf	fly	man
(more than one):	we	us	they	girls	sheaves	flies	men

When we tell whether one or more than one is meant, we give the NUMBER of a noun or pronoun.

The form of a noun or pronoun which shows one person or thing is called the SINGULAR NUMBER. The form of a noun or pronoun which shows more than one person or thing is called the PLURAL NUMBER.

Note that most nouns form their plural by adding *s* or *es* to the singular. We shall study later other ways of forming plurals. The pronoun *you* has the same form for the singular and plural.

We give the person and number of pronominal adjectives, just as we do for pronouns.

EXERCISE 65

Give the person and number of each pronoun in Exercise 62.

EXERCISE 66

Give the kind and number of each noun, and the kind, person, and number of each pronoun in the following:

The trial and death of Socrates, as it has been written by his beloved pupil Plato, is even today one of the masterpieces in the world's history.

It tells how Socrates appeared before his judges, the men of Athens, to answer the charges against himself, and it gives the words of that wonderful defence. Socrates begs for his life, not for his own sake, but for theirs; he is their heaven-sent friend, though they know it not. He is an old man already, and the Athenians will gain nothing by taking away from him the few years of life remaining.

Fearlessly he speaks to his judges of death. "Be of good cheer about death," he cries to the crowded court, "and know of a certainty that no evil can happen to a good man, either in life, or after death. The hour of departure has arrived and we go our ways — I to die and you to live. Which is better, God only knows."

Case in Nouns and Pronouns

Examine the following groups of sentences, and notice the form of the personal pronouns used in them:

1. *I* came home.
   The man saw *me.*
   This is *my* bicycle.

2. *We* rang the bell.
   The man saw *us.*
   That is *our* house.

3. *He* entered the room.
   The teacher greeted *him.*
   It is *his* coat.

4. *They* work here.
   The man praised *them.*
   These are *their* shoes.

In the first group of sentences you see three pronouns — *I, me, my.* These are three forms of the same pronoun. In each of the other groups you also see three forms of the same pronoun. Study the sentences to see if you can find a reason for this.

Why are three forms of the same pronoun needed? To get an answer to that question, give the relation of each pronoun.

From this work we learn:

(1) The subject of the verb in each sentence requires a particular form of the personal pronoun.

(2) The object of the verb in each sentence requires a particular form of the personal pronoun.

(3) The sentence in each group which shows ownership or possession requires a particular form of the pronoun.

You see that these pronouns have different forms to indicate different relations. For instance, *I* is the subject form; *me* is the object form; *my* is the possessive form.

A noun changes its form to show possession, but it has the same form when it is an object as when it is a subject.

When we tell whether a noun or pronoun is used in the sentence as subject, object, or to show possession, we give its CASE. Nouns and pronouns used as subjects are in the NOMINATIVE CASE. Nouns and pronouns used as objects are in the OBJECTIVE CASE. Nouns and pronouns used to show possession are in the POSSESSIVE CASE.

Certain pronouns have two possessive forms, as follows:

my, mine; her, hers; our, ours; your, yours; their, theirs

The first in each pair is always used with a noun, and is called a POSSESSIVE PRONOMINAL ADJECTIVE. The second in each pair is used without a noun, and is called a POSSESSIVE PRONOUN.

Notice that the object of a preposition requires the same form as the object of a verb. It is always in the objective case.

Declension of Pronouns

You have learned that personal pronouns change their form for number, and that they also change their form for case. When we give the forms of a pronoun for number and for case, we DECLINE the pronoun. This we call giving its DECLENSION.

The study of these declensions will teach you when to use each form.

(1) Pronoun *I* of the first person:

	Singular	*Plural*
Nominative:	I	we
Possessive:	my, mine	our, ours
Objective:	me	us

(2) Pronoun *you* of the second person:

	Singular	*Plural*
Nominative:	you	you
Possessive:	your, yours	your, yours
Objective:	you	you

60

(3) Pronouns *he, she, it,* of the third person:

	Singular			Plural	
Nominative:	he	she	it	they	
Possessive:	his	her, hers	its	their, theirs	
Objective:	him	her	it	them	

(4) Declension of the pronoun *who*:

	Singular	Plural
Nominative:	who	who
Possessive:	whose	whose
Objective:	whom	whom

(The forms *thou, thee, thine* (*thy*), and *ye* are omitted, as they are not commonly used.)

Notice that the possessive pronouns *its, hers, theirs, ours, yours,* are written without an apostrophe.

EXERCISE 67

Give orally the case and the relation of each pronoun.

1. Who did that?
2. The dog ran after them.
3. Who came with you?
4. You and he are tall.
5. Whom did you invite?
6. I saw you with them.
7. He knows them well.
8. We ran from them.
9. Whom should I ask?
10. She lost her pen.
11. Who will go for it?
12. I was helping him.
13. Your cousin visited us.
14. Who knows the answer?
15. She and I will go together.
16. I saw her at the show.
17. Whom do you sit with?
18. Who lives in that house?
19. Whom did you buy that for?
20. She and her brother left early.
21. This present is for you and her.
22. Whom are you going with?
23. They know their work well.
24. That money is for him and me.
25. Of whom were you speaking?
26. He and I live on the same street.

Declension of Nouns

Nouns can be declined, but the only changes in form are to indicate the plural and to show the possessive case. To form the possessive of nouns we use an apostrophe and *s* in the singular (*'s*), and an apostrophe after the *s* in the plural (*s'*). You will learn more about possessives later.

For example, study the declension of the noun *boy*:

	Singular	*Plural*
Nominative:	boy	boys
Possessive:	boy's	boys'
Objective:	boy	boys

To give the relation of a possessive noun, simply say that it shows possession of what follows.

Example: The boy's hat is brown.

   boy's — a noun in the possessive case showing the possession of *hat*.

EXERCISE 68

Give orally the case and the relation of each noun.

1. The sun's rays were hot.
2. The campers threw water on the fire.
3. Strange plants grow in tropical countries.
4. Rich men's fortunes were not easily made.
5. The settler's house was small.
6. Some early inhabitants of this earth lived in caves.
7. The hunters saw a flock of wild geese above their heads.
8. The rainbow's colours delight us.
9. The boy's hands were cold.
10. Large cakes of ice floated in the lake.
11. Farmers boiled sap in large kettles.
12. On the peaks of the mountains snow glistened in the bright sunlight.
13. Canada's capital is Ottawa.

Predicate Nominative

A noun or pronoun which follows a copula verb is always in the nominative case. It is called a PREDICATE NOMINATIVE. It completes the predicate and stands for the same person or thing as the subject. See page 34 and notice that the only change is that we now call the predicate noun a predicate nominative.

A predicate nominative, which is always a noun or pronoun, is a SUBJECTIVE COMPLETION. (You will remember that a subjective completion may be an adjective, in which case it is called a predicate adjective.)

The relation of a predicate nominative should be given as follows:

Example: The men are partners. That is he.

   partners — a predicate nominative completing the copula verb *are*, and standing for *men*.

   he - a predicate nominative completing the copula verb *is*, and standing for the person represented by *that*.

EXERCISE 69

Give orally the relation of each predicate nominative.

1. He is a sailor.
2. It is I.
3. I am a teacher.
4. You are a student.
5. It was she.
6. It was he.
7. She is a musician.
8. It was they.
9. Dictators are tyrants.
10. Crows are thieves.
11. He became a skilful doctor.
12. They were good architects.
13. Former enemies now appear good friends.
14. Bees are tireless workers.
15. A dog is a good companion.
16. They are assistants in the library.
17. His great wealth seems a hindrance.
18. Obstacles are often incentives to greater effort.

CHAPTER VII

TENSE IN VERBS

Tense in Verbs

Examine the following sentences and decide whether the action of the verb takes place in the present, past, or future.

1. He *talks* about his work.
   He *talked* about his work.
   He *will talk* about his work.

2. They *know* their lessons.
   They *knew* their lessons.
   They *will know* their lessons.

A study of these sentences shows:

(1) The verb in the first sentence of each group shows PRESENT TIME. The action is happening *now*.

(2) The verb in the second sentence of each group shows PAST TIME. The action is *finished* or completed.

(3) The verb in the third sentence of each group shows FUTURE TIME. The action has not yet taken place, but *will take place* in the future.

(4) The form of the verb for past time is different from the form for present time.

(5) To show future time, an auxiliary verb is used with the form for present time.

The change in the form of a verb to show a change in time is called TENSE. The three tenses shown by these verbs are known as the PRESENT, PAST, and FUTURE TENSES.

We are now ready to write the first person, second person, and third person pronouns with the tense forms of a verb.

Study these tenses of the verb *know*:

	PRESENT TENSE		PAST TENSE	
	Singular	*Plural*	*Singular*	*Plural*
1st Person	I know	we know	I knew	we knew
2nd Person	you know	you know	you knew	you knew
3rd Person	he knows	they know	he knew	they knew

	FUTURE TENSE	
	Singular	*Plural*
1st Person	I shall know	we shall know
2nd Person	you will know	you will know
3rd Person	he will know	they will know

Note: Additional forms of the second person singular are: *thou knowest, thou knewest, thou wilt know.* These are not commonly used.

Study these tenses of the verb *be*:

	PRESENT TENSE		PAST TENSE	
	Singular	*Plural*	*Singular*	*Plural*
1st Person	I am	we are	I was	we were
2nd Person	you are	you are	you were	you were
3rd Person	he is	they are	he was	they were

	FUTURE TENSE	
	Singular	*Plural*
1st Person	I shall be	we shall be
2nd Person	you will be	you will be
3rd Person	he will be	they will be

EXERCISE 70

Write the present, past, and future tense forms of the following verbs:

write, run, go, find, think

Special Uses of the Future Tense

In the future tense, the auxiliary *shall* is used in the first person, and the auxiliary *will* is used in the second and third persons. This is called the SIMPLE FUTURE. The simple future shows what is expected to happen.

Study these sentences.

1. I *will* never *reveal* your plans.
2. "I *will have* that mouse," said the little kitten.
3. "You *shall* not *have* that mouse," said the bigger one.
4. He *shall* not *remain* here.
5. They *shall* not *pass*.

In these sentences the uses of the auxiliaries *shall* and *will* are exactly reversed from those in the simple future. *Will* is used in the first person, and *shall* is used in the second and third persons. This use of *shall* and *will* is called the FUTURE OF PROMISE OR DETERMINATION. The speaker uses it to give a promise or express determination.

We have this rule for the uses of *shall* and *will*. To show the simple future, use *shall* in the first person and *will* in the second and third persons. To show the future of promise or determination, use *will* in the first person and *shall* in the second and third persons.

EXERCISE 71

State whether the verb shows the simple future, or the future of promise or determination.

1. I shall probably go.
2. I will not listen to you.
3. He will treat you well.
4. We will wait for you.
5. They will expect us.
6. I shall try again.
7. We shall phone tomorrow.
8. Their work will please you.

9. We will never yield to the enemy.
10. They shall not receive help from me.
11. I will aid you in every possible way.
12. We shall not pass this way again.
13. You will enjoy the concert.
14. He will not come home.
15. You shall remain at home.
16. She shall never have my consent.
17. We shall have a pleasant afternoon.
18. I shall be glad to assist you.
19. You will know him by his walk.
20. I will do it, and nothing shall stop me.

Agreement between Subject and Predicate

Singular	*Plural*
1. I *am* at school.	We *are* at school.
2. You *are* at school.	You *are* at school.
3. He *is* at school.	They *are* at school.

In these sentences, a particular form of the verb must be used with each pronoun, although in some cases the same form of the verb is used with different subjects.

Notice the different forms of the verb. With the pronoun in the first person singular, we use *am*; with the pronoun in the third person singular, we use *is*; with the pronoun in the third person plural, we use *are*. In these sentences, as the subject changes in form to show a change in person and number, the form of the verb changes. This change is known as AGREEMENT BETWEEN SUBJECT AND PREDICATE. We say that a verb agrees with its subject in person and number.

The verb *be*, which is shown above in the present tense, has more changes for agreement between subject and predicate than any other verb. With other verbs, the change is mainly in the third person singular of the present tense. This is shown by the verbs in the following sentences:

I *do* not remember his name.
You *do* not remember his name.
He *does* not remember his name.

We *do* not remember his name.
You *do* not remember his name.
They *do* not remember his name.

The change in the form of the verb for number also takes place when a noun is the subject.

Example: The boy *writes*. The boys *write*.

We must always use a plural form of the verb when the subject is a plural noun or pronoun. Also, a plural form of the verb must be used with a compound subject, as: The boy and his sister *come* to school.

A good way to learn agreement between subject and predicate is to practise using the correct form of the verb in sentences.

EXERCISE 72

In the following sentences, choose the correct form of the verb:

1. We (*was, were*) at school today.
2. He (*don't, doesn't*) live on his farm.
3. Accidents (*happens, happen*) too frequently.
4. I (*like, likes*) your hat.
5. There (*was, were*) thousands of people at the Exhibition.
6. Hail and frost often (*injure, injures*) the fruit crops.
7. These seats (*is, are*) too far back.
8. Those boys (*plays, play*) in our school orchestra.

9. (*Was, were*) your answer correct?
10. I (*go, goes*) to church on Sunday.
11. They (*do, does*) the chores every day.
12. The girls (*have, has*) prepared a lunch.
13. There (*was, were*) two children on the road.
14. Dandelions (*grow, grows*) on our lawn.
15. The little girls (*was, were*) very noisy.
16. You and I (*go, goes*) to the same dentist.
17. The votes (*was, were*) all counted.
18. Many of the neighbours (*has, have*) gone to the picnic.
19. Who (*was, were*) those men in the car?
20. At the door (*sit, sits*) Dick and Tom.
21. (*Was, were*) you the first speaker?
22. Blanche and her sister (*take, takes*) the bus every night.
23. Robert and his friends (*is, are*) here.

EXERCISE 73

Give the tense, the person, and the number of each verb.

1. He always carried a book in his pocket.
2. We rise early in the morning.
3. They will not see him again.
4. I recognized you at once.
5. The boys answered the questions promptly.
6. I shall always respect him.
7. The explorers hunted lions in Africa.
8. The horses pull well together.
9. You will never be without friends.
10. The boat skims over the water.
11. They were good neighbours.
12. She will not know you.
13. He has good judgment.
14. We shall be there early.
15. Missionaries risked their lives in foreign countries.
16. The painter works rapidly.

The Perfect Tenses

Examine the following sentences, and decide at what time the action takes place:

I *have finished* my work.
You *have finished* your work.
He *has finished* his work.

In each sentence the verb indicates an action which has been completed in a time very close to the present, and the auxiliaries *have* and *has* are used with the principal verb. This is called the PRESENT PERFECT TENSE.

Now examine the following sentences, and consider the time of the verbs:

I *had finished* my work before noon.
You *had finished* your work before noon.
He *had finished* his work before noon.

In each sentence the verb indicates an action which was completed prior to another time or another action, and the auxiliary *had* is used with the principal verb. This is called the PAST PERFECT TENSE.

Next examine the following sentences, and consider the time of the verb:

I *shall have finished* my work by noon tomorrow.
You *will have finished* your work by noon tomorrow.
He *will have finished* his work by noon tomorrow.

In each sentence the verb indicates an action which will be completed before some point of time in the future, and the auxiliaries *shall have* and *will have* are used with the principal verb. This is called the FUTURE PERFECT TENSE.

You will find it easy to recognize perfect tenses from the use of the auxiliary verb *have* in its various forms.

70

Conjugation of Verbs

When we give the tense forms of a verb with the first, second, and third person pronouns, we CONJUGATE the verb. You have already done this for the present, past, and future tenses.

Here is the conjugation of the verb *see* in the **present** perfect, past perfect, and future perfect tenses.

PRESENT PERFECT TENSE

	Singular	*Plural*
1st Person	I have seen	we have seen
2nd Person	you have seen	you have seen
3rd Person	he has seen	they have seen

PAST PERFECT TENSE

	Singular	*Plural*
1st Person	I had seen	we had seen
2nd Person	you had seen	you had seen
3rd Person	he had seen	they had seen

FUTURE PERFECT TENSE

	Singular	*Plural*
1st Person	I shall have seen	we shall have seen
2nd Person	you will have seen	you will have seen
3rd Person	he will have seen	they will have seen

Perfect Tenses of the Verb *be*

On page 65 we conjugated the verb *be* in the present, past, and future tenses. Here is the conjugation of the verb *be* in the present perfect, past perfect, and future perfect tenses.

PRESENT PERFECT TENSE

	Singular	*Plural*
1st Person	I have been	we have been
2nd Person	you have been	you have been
3rd Person	he has been	they have been

PAST PERFECT TENSE

	Singular	*Plural*
1st Person	I had been	we had been
2nd Person	you had been	you had been
3rd Person	he had been	they had been

FUTURE PERFECT TENSE

	Singular	*Plural*
1st Person	I shall have been	we shall have been
2nd Person	you will have been	you will have been
3rd Person	he will have been	they will have been

Principal Parts of the Verb

The form of the principal verb which is used in the perfect tenses is called the PAST PARTICIPLE. In the sentence, *I have written*, for example, *written* is the past participle.

The present tense form, the past tense form, and the past participle are called the PRINCIPAL PARTS OF THE VERB. The principal parts of some verbs are given here, but you should consult the appendix of this book and your dictionary for the principal parts of other verbs.

Present Tense	Past Tense	Past Participle	Present Tense	Past Tense	Past Participle
begin	began	begun	lie (*to recline*)	lay	lain
bite	bit	bitten			
break	broke	broken	raise	raised	raised
bring	brought	brought	ring	rang	rung
burn	burned *or* burnt	burned *or* burnt	rise	rose	risen
			run	ran	run
come	came	come	saw	sawed	sawed *or* sawn
do	did	done			
draw	drew	drawn	see	saw	seen
drive	drove	driven	sell	sold	sold
eat	ate *or* eat *	eaten	set	set	set
			shake	shook	shaken
fall	fell	fallen	show	showed	shown *or* showed
fly	flew	flown			
get	got	got *or* gotten	sing	sang	sung
			sit	sat	sat
give	gave	given	stand	stood	stood
go	went	gone	take	took	taken
grow	grew	grown	throw	threw	thrown
know	knew	known	wear	wore	worn
lay (*to place*)	laid	laid	write	wrote	written

* pronounced "et".

(a) Write from memory the principal parts of the following verbs:

begin	fly	know	see	tell
come	get	lay	send	throw
do	give	lie	set	write
drain	go	raise	take	
drive	grow	rise	speak	

(b) Write the conjugation of the verbs *tell* and *send* in the present perfect, past perfect, and future perfect tenses.

(c) Write the conjugation of the verb *be* (*am*) in the present, past, future, present perfect, past perfect, and future perfect tenses.

(d) Give orally the conjugation of the verbs *do*, *lie*, and *lay* in the six tenses.

(a) Write the following tense forms of the verb *speak*:

    i. third person plural, past tense
    ii. first person singular, present tense
    iii. second person plural, future tense
    iv. third person singular, future perfect tense
    v. first person plural, present perfect tense
    vi. third person singular, past perfect tense
    vii. first person plural, future tense
    viii. second person singular, future perfect tense
    ix. third person singular, present perfect tense
    x. third person singular, future tense
    xi. second person plural, past tense
    xii. first person singular, past perfect tense
    xiii. second person singular, present perfect tense

(b) Write the following tense forms of the verb *give*:

   i. second person plural, present, perfect tense
  ii. third person singular, future tense
 iii. first person singular, future perfect tense
 iv. second person singular, past perfect tense
   v. third person plural, future tense
 vi. first person plural, future tense
 vii. first person plural, past tense
viii. third person singular, present perfect tense
 ix. third person singular, future perfect tense
   x. first person singular, present tense
 xi. third person plural, past perfect tense
 xii. first person singular, present perfect tense

(c) Write the conjugation of the verbs *take*, *go*, and *write* in the present perfect, past perfect, and future perfect tenses.

(d) Give orally the conjugation of the verbs *rise*, *raise*, and *sing* in the six tenses.

EXERCISE 76

Give the tense, person, number, and relation of each verb in the following sentences:

Example: He pitched well in that game.

> *pitched* — verb, past tense, third person, singular number, having for its subject the pronoun *he*.

1. I shall remain at home.
2. The Indian had run the rapids many times.
3. We shall have finished the work before that time.
4. The pupils had lowered the flag at noon.
5. She will be glad to see you.
6. We have not played with this ball before.
7. They will have gone before evening.
8. On several occasions Byrd had sailed for the Antarctic.
9. For a whole week the ship held to its course.

10. By this time tomorrow I shall have left here.
11. They had decided to go home.
12. I have been there many times.
13. Flames leaped upward into the sky.
14. He has lain there for some time.
15. Friends will meet us at the station.
16. They have given their services freely.
17. Before the great fire London had suffered from a plague.
18. She works in an insurance office.

CHAPTER VIII

SPEAKING AND WRITING CORRECTLY

You are beginning the work of an important chapter. The study of grammar shows how to speak and write correctly. You have learned some rules, and now you are to put them into practice.

The work here will help you to form good speech habits. If you are careful to watch your language, you will soon form the habit of speaking correctly.

Correct Use of Verbs

LIE, LAY

The word *lie* shows a state or position. The word *lay* shows an action. *Lie* means *to recline, to remain in a flat position.* It is an intransitive verb and cannot take an object Its principal parts are: *lie, lay, lain.*

Examples: Occasionally I *lie* on the couch.

Yesterday I *lay* in the sun.

That book *has lain* on my desk for several days.

Special Uses are:

The prairies *lie* in the western part of Canada.

The responsibility *lies* with you.

Lay means *to place.* Its principal parts are: *lay, laid, laid.* It is a transitive verb and takes an object.

Examples: I *lay* things away carefully.

When school closed I *laid* my books away.

I have just *laid* my gloves down.

Special Uses are:

Grasshoppers *laid* bare the fields.

He *laid* claim to the insurance.

Notice that you cannot *lie* anything down, but you can *lay* it down. You cannot *lay* down to sleep, but you can *lie* down to sleep.

RISE, RAISE

Rise means *to move upwards*. It is an intransitive verb. Its principal parts are: *rise, rose, risen.*

Examples: We *rise* early in the morning.
The plane *rose* high into the sky.
He *has risen* to speak.

Special Uses are:
The rebels *rose* in revolt.
He *has risen* in society.
The mountains *rise* to a great height.

Raise means *to lift upwards*. It is a transitive verb. Its principal parts are: *raise, raised, raised.*

Examples: He *raises* his head.
They *have raised* the flag.

Special Uses are:
We *raised* his salary.
That man *raised* a large family.
Canada *raised* an army.

Notice that you *raise* the pans from the table to put them into the oven, but the dough *rises.*

SIT, SET

Sit means *to rest in a sitting position.* Its principal parts are: *sit, sat, sat.* It is generally an intransitive verb.

Examples: The pupils *sit* in seats.
They *sat* on the ground.
They have *sat* there for a long time.

Special Uses are:
The council *sits* every month.
He *sits* in the legislature for our constituency.

Set means *to put in a certain place or position.* Its principal parts are: *set, set, set.* It is generally a transitive verb, but in the fifth example it is used as an intransitive.

Examples: Set the kettle on the stove.

Yesterday you *set* the kettle on the stove.

Have you *set* the kettle on the stove?

Special Uses are:

They have *set* a time for the meeting.

The sun *sets* in the west.

Notice that you *set* dishes on the table, but the dishes *sit* on the table.

EXERCISE 77

Write out the sentences, filling the blanks with the proper forms of *lie* and *lay*.

1. Yesterday I................. on the couch in the morning.
2. The cows have................in the shade for a long time.
3. ....the mat at the door.
4. Usually I.................on my right side.
5. Shall I.................your book on the desk?
6. The bricklayer.................the bricks evenly.
7. He had.................his hat on the bench.
8. The newsboy.................our paper inside the door.
9. The town.................in a pleasant valley.
10. He always.................the blame on others.
11. Last night I.................awake for an hour.
12. He has.................his books down.

EXERCISE 78

Write out the sentences, filling the blanks with the proper forms of *rise* and *raise*.

1. The sun......... ......early in June.
2. They.................him to his feet.
3. I always.................the window at night.
4. Many people.................in rebellion.

79

5. They..............the boat from the bottom of the lake.
6. The water..............during the night.
7. The children have..............money for the Red Cross.
8. The moon has...............
9. The mountains..............high into the sky.
10. I..............early this morning to study.
11. His employer..............his salary.
12. Dairy workers..............early to deliver milk.
13. They had..............the price of butter.
14. The mist has..............from the valley.

EXERCISE 79

Write out the sentences, filling in the blanks with the proper forms of *sit* and *set*.

1. In the tepee Indians..............on the floor.
2. Did you..............the hen?
3. He has..............there all night.
4. He had..............the pail down.
5. The trapper..............his traps in the woods.
6. Shall I..............the chairs around the table?
7. I often..............before the fireplace.
8. Who..............the price of cheese?
9. He..............the basket on the floor.
10. Have you ever..............in the gallery before?
11. He had..............in parliament for many years.
12. ....that box here.
13. Where do you..............?
14. The sun..............behind a cloud.
15. They..............out on a long journey.

BRING, FETCH

Bring means *to carry from where you are. Fetch* means *to go and bring. Bring* implies going *one* way; *fetch* implies going *two* ways.

Examples: Bring your coat tomorrow.

Fetch a pail of water from the well.

CAN, MAY

Can means *to be able*, and is an auxiliary verb. *May* is used *when permission is asked or granted*, and is also an auxiliary verb. *May* is also used *to express possibility*, as in the last three examples.

Examples: I *can* solve the problem.
They *can* succeed.
May I sit here?
You *may* have my pen.
It *may* rain today.
We *may* not arrive until late.
We *may* have a holiday tomorrow.

BEGAN, BEGUN

These are the past tense and past participle forms of the verb *begin*. The use of *begun* in the past tense is a common error. Use *begun* only in the perfect tenses.

Examples: I *began* the lesson this morning.
I have *begun* the lesson.

COME, CAME, COME

These are the principal parts of the verb *come*. Notice that the present tense and past participle forms are similar. Never use *come* in the past tense.

Examples: I *come* to school every day.
I *came* yesterday.
I have *come* for a visit.

DID, DONE

These are the past tense and past participle forms of the verb *do*. The use of *done* in the past tense is a common error. *Done* is always used with an auxiliary verb.

Examples: I *did* the chores.
I have *done* the chores.

Doesn't is the shortened form of *does not*. It requires a subject in the singular number. *Don't* is the shortened form of *do not*. It generally requires a subject in the plural number.

Examples: The clock *doesn't* strike.

These flowers *don't* bloom early.

The following are exceptions to this rule: *I don't*, and *you* (singular) *don't*.

EXERCISE 80

Write out the sentences, completing each with the correct word in brackets. In each case be prepared to give the reason for your choice.

1. I always................my lunch to school. (bring, fetch)
2. We................some new work today. (began, begun)
3. He................write plainly. (don't, doesn't)
4. I................all the chores before supper. (did, done)
5. You have................your story with a good sentence. (begun, began)
6. Please................some wood from the basement. (bring, fetch)
7. We................ here last week for a picnic. (came, come)
8. Grandmother................all her own housework. (done, did)
9. We had................home early. (come, came)
10. Do not................so many books home from the library. (bring, fetch)
11. That hat................suit me. (doesn't, don't)
12. The players................the game late. (begun, began)
13. ....I borrow your coat? (may, can)
14. They................on the train yesterday. (come, came)
15. I had just................my music lesson. (begun, began)
16. He................come here often. (doesn't, don't)
17. I................my homework at school. (did, done)

82

Write out the sentences, filling in the blanks with *may* or *can.*

1. ....I use your telephone?
2. I................never remember his name.
3. You................borrow my book.
4. He................play the accordion.
5. She................name many birds.
6. ....I show my answer?
7. I................see your purpose.
8. This new automobile................travel seventy miles an hour.
9. ....we cross the street at recess, please?
10. I................do all the questions.
11. Foxes................run fast.
12. ....I have another sandwich?
13. He................play the piano well.
14. This................be your last chance.
15. ....I see your mother?
16. ....he sing well?
17. ....my father ride in your car?

GIVE, GAVE, GIVEN

These are the principal parts of the verb *give*. The use of *give* in the past tense is a common error. Use *given* in the perfect tenses.

Examples: I *give* regularly to the Red Cross.

I *gave* my report yesterday.

I have *given* my report.

KNEW, KNOWN

These are the past tense and past participle forms of the verb *know*. Use *knew* in the past tense, and *known* in the perfect tenses. (There is no such word as *knowed*.)

Examples: I *knew* that last year.

I have *known* that for a long time.

SAW, SEEN

These are the past tense and past participle forms of the verb *see*. Never use *seen* in the past tense.

Examples: I *saw* the picture.
I have *seen* the picture.
I had *seen* the picture.

SHALL, WILL

To show the simple future, use *shall* in the first person and *will* in the second and third persons. To show the future of promise or determination, reverse this use. This has been dealt with previously on page 66.

TEACH, LEARN

Teach means *to instruct*. *Learn* means *to acquire knowledge*, and never to impart it.

Examples: He *teaches* them grammar.
They *learn* grammar.

WENT, GONE

These are the past tense and past participle forms of the verb *go*. *Went* should never be used in the perfect tenses.

Examples: I *went* there.
I have *gone* there.
You had *gone* there.
She will have *gone* there.

EXERCISE 82

Write out the sentences, completing each with the correct word in brackets. In each case be prepared to give the reason for your choice.

1. I certainly................not give my consent. (will, shall)
2. I................you my answer yesterday. (give, gave)
3. He................his dog to sit up. (learned, taught)

4. We................a television set in the store. (seen, saw)
5. They................probably come here tomorrow. (shall, will)
6. I have................the same recitation before. (given, gave)
7. Our friends had................for a visit. (gone, went)
8. He................my answer. (seen, saw)
9. They................all about it. (knew, knowed)
10. I................never forget my first attempt to swim. (will, shall)
11. He has just................away. (gone, went)
12. Many people have................better days. (saw, seen)
13. I................to school every day last year. (come, came)
14. Do not................on the damp ground. (lie, lay)
15. He................others to drive the tractor. (teaches, learns)
16. We................you in the store. (saw, seen)

EXERCISE 83

Write out the sentences, completing each with the correct word in brackets. In each case be prepared to give the reason for your choice.

1. I have................a car for two years. (drove, driven)
2. I hope you................have a good time at the party. (shall, will)
3. They had................the lock on the door. (broken, broke)
4. Your explanation................satisfy me. (doesn't, don't)
5. These potatoes................very small. (is, are)
6. I................never alter my decision. (will, shall)
7. The boy and his sister................sick. (is, are)
8. They................all the way home yesterday. (run, ran)
9. He has................his books away. (took, taken)
10. My brother and I................often at their home. (were, was)
11. You................receive my reply at once. (will, shall)
12. He has................several books. (written, wrote)
13. You and I................very fortunate. (was, were)
14. We................you at the Exhibition Grounds. (saw, seen)
15. They................many old songs. (sung, sang)
16. The berries in this pail................small. (is, are)

Watch These Prepositions

BESIDE, BESIDES

Beside means *at the side of. Besides* means *in addition to.*

Examples: He placed his bat *beside* the bench.
He thinks of others *besides* himself.

BETWEEN, AMONG

In referring to two, use *between*. In referring to more than two, use *among*.

Examples: This secret is *between* you and me.
He divided the profits *among* the workers.

Notice that it is a glaring error to use the nominative form of the pronoun, *I*, instead of the objective form, *me*, after the preposition *between*. Never say: between you and I.

IN, INTO

The preposition *in* shows a position within or inside. The preposition *into* shows movement from without to a position within.

Examples: He studies *in* his room.
He came *into* my office.

OF, OFF

Of is a preposition. *Off* is a preposition, an adverb, and an adjective. Do not use *off* and *of* together. It is wrong to say: He came *off of* the train. The correct statement is: He came *off* the train. Consult your dictionary for the other uses of the word *off*.

Note: Never use *of* instead of the auxiliary verb *have*. Say: You should *have* received the prize. Do not say: You should *of* received the prize.

Write out the sentences, completing each with the correct word in brackets. In each case be prepared to give the reason for your choice.

1. He walked................the house ahead of me. (in, into)
2. ....his board he received a small salary. (besides, beside)
3. This is a secret................him and me. (among, between)
4. Bears are fond................honey. (of, off)
5. She burst hurriedly................the room. (in, into)
6. Much snow fell................the roof. (off of, off)
7. You should................gone. (of, have)
8. Divide all the prizes................the three winners. (among, between)
9. They stuffed candies................the Christmas stockings. (in, into)
10. We ate lunch................the stream. (besides, beside)
11. The boys walked................together. (of, off)
12. He thrust his hand................the mitt. (into, in)
13. The man divided his fortune................his five sons. (between, among)
14. He might................come with us. (of, have)
15. They moved................that house yesterday. (into, in)

Watch These Pronouns

ONE	ANYONE	NO ONE	EVERYONE	SOMEONE
EACH	ANYBODY	NOBODY	EVERYBODY	SOMEBODY

These indefinite pronouns are singular in number, and they require singular verbs. Another pronoun in the sentence which refers to one of these words must be in the singular number.

Examples: Each of us is willing to do *his* share.
Everyone has *his* ticket.
Did *anybody* lose *his* fountain pen?

EITHER, NEITHER

Either and *neither* are indefinite pronouns. Do not use these words in referring to more than two, and always use a singular verb with each word.

Examples: Either of them is able to do that.
Neither of the pupils knows the answer.

I, WE, HE, SHE, THEY

These pronouns must always be used in the nominative case.

Examples: They and *we* will go at the same time.
She and *he* were away.
He and *I* went together.

ITS, IT'S

The possessive form of the pronoun *it* is *its*, and does not require an apostrophe. *It's* is the shortened form of *it is*.

Examples: The kitten licked *its* paws.
It's time to leave.

ME, US, HIM, HER, THEM

Use these pronouns in the objective case. Note that *her* is also a possessive pronominal adjective.

Examples: Let us divide the cake between *them* and *us.*
Will you telephone to *him* and *her?*
My dog will do many tricks for *me.*

THEIR, THEIRS, THERE, THERE'S

Their is a possessive pronominal adjective. The possessive pronoun is *theirs*, which does not take an apostrophe. *There* is an adverb and an expletive. *There's* is the shortened form of *there is*.

Examples: There is *their* house.
There's no other farm like *theirs* in the district.

You takes a plural verb whether it stands for one, or more than one. It never takes a singular verb. (There is no such word as *youse*.)

Examples: Are *you* a carpenter?
You are good citizens.

WHO, WHOM

Always use *who* in the nominative case, and *whom* in the objective case.

Examples: Who called me?
Whom are you expecting?
Whom did you wave to?

EXERCISE 85

Write out the sentences, completing each with the correct word or words in brackets. In each case be prepared to give the reason for your choice.

1. Neither he nor I................there. (were, was)
2. This book is................. (yours, your's)
3. The children and................ ....having a good time. (he, him; is, are)
4. Either Mary or Jane................ ....coat on my hook. (have, has; their, her)
5. ....do you see? (who, whom)
6. The bus will wait for you and................. (I, me)
7. Everybody must pay................taxes. (his, their)
8. It wasn't................. (I, me)
9. ....and................frequently................on the boat. (he, him; me, I; were, was)
10. I never could see................use. (its, it's)
11. ....anybody seen my sweater? (has, have)
12. I bought this car for................and her mother. (she, her)
13. ....either of you seen my keys? (has, have)
14. Not one of these answers................correct. (are, is)

15. Either of these roads................to the city. (leads, lead)
16. Everyone should know................neighbours. (his, their)
17. John and................will help you. (me, I)
18. Neither of the windows................tightly. (shut, shuts)
19. All of the stores................in the evenings. (close, closes)
20. ....names are difficult to pronounce. (there, their)
21. ....are you waiting for? (who, whom)
22. ....and................generally................. (her, she; I, me; agrees, agree)
23. These books are................. (their's, theirs)
24. Either time................convenient for me. (are, is)

Correct Use of Adverbs and Adjectives

A word modifying a noun or pronoun is an adjective, while a word modifying a verb, adjective, or adverb is an adverb. You will remember that the copula verbs *feel, smell, sound, taste, look,* are followed by predicate adjectives.

GOOD, WELL

Good is always an adjective. *Well* is generally an adverb, but it is an adjective when it means *in good health.*

Examples: He played *well*; he sang *well*. (adverbs)
He looks *well*. (adjective meaning *healthy*, modifying *he*)

EXERCISE 86

Write out the sentences, completing each with the correct word in brackets. In each case be prepared to give the reason for your choice.

1. The child does not feel................. (good, well)
2. The cookies smell................. (well, good)
3. He swims and dives................. (well, good)
4. He does not write................. (plain, plainly)

5. She sings................ (beautiful, beautifully)
6. Your skates feel................ (sharply, sharp)
7. The mechanic spoke...............about his invention. (confidently, confident)
8. The cake tastes................ (well, good)
9. Birds sing...............in the spring. (sweetly, sweet)
10. The stranger spoke very................ (earnest, earnestly)
11. Your explanation sounds...............to me. (strange, strangely)
12. Hounds smell................ (keen, keenly)
13. That man always looks................ (sad, sadly)
14. Don't you feel...............in this place? (queer, queerly)
15. The bell tolled very................ (faintly, faint)
16. The general looked...............at the soldiers. (close, closely).
17. The taxi-drivers sounded their horns................ (loudly, loud)
18. The barber felt the edge of the razor................ (careful, carefully)
19. The milk tastes................ (sourly, sour)
20. Drive................ (careful, carefully)

REVIEW—Correct Usage

EXERCISE 87

Choose the right word in each sentence and state your reason.

1. (*Who, whom*) do you prefer for the position?
2. How many of you (*fetched, brought*) a lunch?
3. He is a (*really, real*) famous man.
4. Do not put paper (*in, into*) the stove.
5. I have never (*drove, driven*) over this road before.
6. Your garden is growing (*well, good*).
7. This clock (*don't, doesn't*) keep good time.
8. That road looks (*badly, bad*).
9. Neither of the two days (*are, is*) suitable to me.
10. The mat was (*laying, lying*) at the front door.

11. The boy was (*sitting, setting*) on his cap.
12. The successful pupils (*shall, will*) receive their certificates soon.
13. The water in the lake (*rises, raises*) after a heavy rain.
14. The children have (*gone, went*) to school.
15. (*Brightly, bright*) coloured flowers make an attractive bouquet.
16. I (*seen, saw*) several strange birds.
17. The judge (*give, gave*) the man another chance.
18. They (*was, were*) ready for the bus.
19. (*May, can*) we use your boat?
20. The river meanders (*lazily, lazy*) through the meadow.
21. You should (*of, have*) seen the circus.
22. The pupils behaved (*well, good*) at the game.
23. (*Were, was*) either of your parents there?
24. It is a long (*way, ways*) through the tunnel.

CHAPTER IX

NOUNS

Plurals in Nouns, Possessive Case, Gender

Formation of Plurals in Nouns

1. Most nouns form their plural by adding *s* or *es*.

   apple, apples; box, boxes; brush, brushes.

2. Nouns ending in *y* preceded by a vowel form their plural by adding *s*.

   day, days; turkey, turkeys; toy, toys.

   Nouns ending in *y* preceded by a consonant form their plural by changing the *y* to *i* and adding *es*.

   city, cities; lady, ladies; country, countries.

3. Nouns ending in *o* preceded by a vowel form their plural by adding *s*.

   folio, folios; radio, radios; cuckoo, cuckoos.

   Nouns ending in *o* preceded by a consonant usually form their plural by adding *es*.

   potato, potatoes; hero, heroes; echo, echoes.

   Note: Musical terms, and a few other words which end in *o* preceded by a consonant, add only *s*.

   piano, pianos; solo, solos; soprano, sopranos;
   rondo, rondos; banjo, banjos.

4. Some nouns ending in *f* or *fe* change the *f* to *v* and add *es* or *s*.

   loaf, loaves; leaf, leaves; wife, wives.

5. A few nouns form their plural by a vowel change within the word.

   man, men; tooth, teeth; mouse, mice.

6. A few nouns use *n* or *en* to form their plural.

> child, children; ox, oxen.

7. Some nouns which come from foreign languages have their foreign plurals.

> basis, bases; curriculum, curricula; datum, data;
> larva, larvæ; phenomenon, phenomena;
> radius, radii; stratum, strata; tableau, tableaux.

8. Compound nouns usually pluralize the more important word.

> father-in-law, fathers-in-law; governor-general,
> governors-general; lieutenant-governor, lieutenant-
> governors.

Note: A few compound nouns pluralize both parts.

> man-servant, men-servants.

9. Some nouns are plural in form but singular in meaning, and require a singular verb.

> news, mumps, measles, civics.

Example: The *news* was good.

Other nouns are always plural, and require a plural verb.

> scissors, ashes, trousers, tongs, riches, thanks.

Example: Riches do not always bring happiness.

10. Letters, figures, and words used merely as words, form their plural by adding an apostrophe and *s*.

> c's, 9's, and's.

Examples: Your *c's* and your *9's* are not legible.

> Avoid the use of so many *and's.*

11. A few nouns have the same form in the singular and plural.

> deer, moose, salmon, trout, Iroquois, sheep.

12. Some nouns have two plural forms.

> brother, brothers, brethren; penny, pennies, pence.

Write the following words in a column, and beside each write its plural:

axis	cliff	piano	crisis	knife	pailful
solo	negro	radio	tomato	if	formula
fife	goose	banjo	wharf	valley	man-of-war
so	sheaf	child	motto	soprano	maid-servant

Give the singular of each of the following:

wives	wolves	allies	larvae	remedies	moneys
feet	folios	shelves	echoes	spoonfuls	potatoes
ways	oases	ponies	factories	tableaux	sons-in-law
lice	beaux	leaves	thieves	chimneys	storeys
roofs	strata	parties	glories	baths	women-
8's	two's	cantos	calves	wrenches	servants
lives	oxen	cargoes	stories	volcanoes	

Write each sentence, using the correct word in italics.

1. The news (*is, are*) good.
2. The lumps of sugar (*is, are*) hard.
3. The (*axes, axis*) of the earth is an imaginary line joining the poles.
4. The scissors (*was, were*) sharp.
5. The (*oases, oasis*) are often far apart in the desert.
6. Take two (*spoons full, spoonfuls*) of this medicine.
7. Mathematics (*is, are*) an easy subject for some students.
8. The (*tableau, tableaux*) was well acted.
9. Mumps (*is, are*) an infectious disease.
10. Ashes (*was, were*) used with fat to make soap.
11. (*This, these*) larva (*is, are*) very small.
12. Several boxes of candy (*was, were*) on the shelf.
13. (*This, these*) phenomena (*is, are*) unusual in winter.
14. In this quarry notice several (*layer, layers*) of limestone.

Possessive Case in Nouns

1. To form the possessive case of singular nouns we add an apostrophe and *s*.

>girl's book, John's hat, dog's collar.

Note: In the case of a few singular nouns which have two *s* sounds, only the apostrophe is added. The addition of another *s* sound would make these words difficult to pronounce.

>conscience' sake, Moses' laws.

2. To form the possessive case of plural nouns not ending in *s*, we add an apostrophe and *s*.

>women's, children's, oxen's.

3. To form the possessive case of plural nouns ending in *s*, we add only the apostrophe.

>girls', ladies', officers'.

4. The possessive case of compound nouns is formed by adding an apostrophe and *s* to the last word.

>son-in-law's, sisters-in-law's, men-of-war's.

5. The idea of possession for things that are not living is often expressed by a phrase beginning with the preposition *of*. This usually sounds more pleasing than using the word with an apostrophe.

>the end of the road, the roof of the house,
>the streets of the town.

With nouns indicating *time* the apostrophe and *s* are usually used.

>an hour's delay, a month's notice, one year's
>interest, a day's work.

Write the possessive singular and possessive plural of each of the following nouns:

man	ox	woman	sister	editor	merchant
bird	wolf	actor	friend	family	giraffe
wife	child	gypsy	lawyer	mother	monkey
hero	week	enemy	teacher	turkey	mother-in-law

Gender in Nouns

Nouns which represent a male being are of the MASCULINE GENDER, and nouns which represent a female being are of the FEMININE GENDER. Nouns which may be either masculine or feminine are said to be of COMMON GENDER, as:

child, bird, cousin.

Nouns which represent objects without life are of the NEUTER GENDER.

chair, box, house, hill.

However, we frequently speak of certain inanimate objects as if they had gender. For example, *ship*, *moon*, *nature*, are often referred to as *she*. In other languages you may study, you will find that objects without life are often of masculine or feminine gender.

Nouns of the opposite gender are shown in the following ways:

1. By the use of different words.

king	man	husband	uncle
queen	woman	wife	aunt
monk	father	nephew	youth
nun	mother	niece	maiden
master	goose		
mistress	gander		

2. By the addition of an ending to the masculine.

actor	baron	count	deacon
actress	baroness	countess	deaconess

god	heir	hero	tiger
goddess	heiress	heroine	tigress

lion	patron	prince	host
lioness	patroness	princess	hostess

3. By changing one part of a compound noun.

he-wolf	man-servant	landlord
she-wolf	maid-servant	landlady

EXERCISE 92

State the gender of each noun, and give its opposite gender. Before beginning, study gender forms in the Appendix.

lad	duck	goose	widow	actor	daughter
nun	mare	vixen	master	prophet	shepherd
hen	heir	baron	bride	tigress	bachelor
cow	duke	youth	deacon	heroine	princess
ewe	lord	uncle	waiter	hostess	maid-servant

CHAPTER X

ADJECTIVES AND ADVERBS

Comparison of Adjectives and Adverbs

Comparison of Adjectives

Examine the words in italics in the following sentences:

Monday was a *cold* day.

Tuesday was a *colder* day than Monday.

Wednesday was the *coldest* day of the three.

Here you see three forms of the adjective *cold*, which are used to show different degrees of coldness. When we change the form of adjectives in this way, we COMPARE them, or give their COMPARISON.

In the above sentences three different degrees of the same quality are expressed. The adjective *cold* is said to be in the POSITIVE DEGREE. The adjective *colder* is formed by adding *er* to the positive degree, and it is said to be in the COMPARATIVE DEGREE. The adjective *coldest* is formed by adding *est* to the positive degree, and it is said to be in the SUPERLATIVE DEGREE.

The comparative and superlative degrees of adjectives are formed in three ways.

1. The first way of forming the comparative and superlative degrees of adjectives is by using *er* or *r* with the positive to form the comparative, and *est* or *st* with the positive to form the superlative. This is called REGULAR COMPARISON. This method is used with adjectives of one

syllable, and with adjectives of two syllables when the comparative and superlative forms are easily pronounced.

Positive	Comparative	Superlative
large	larger	largest
bright	brighter	brightest
happy	happier	happiest
noble	nobler	noblest
strong	stronger	strongest
pretty	prettier	prettiest
wealthy	wealthier	wealthiest
lazy	lazier	laziest
quiet	quieter	quietest
clever	cleverer	cleverest

2. The second way of forming the comparative and superlative degrees of adjectives is by placing in front of the positive form the adverbs *more* and *most*, or *less* and *least*. This is called PHRASAL COMPARISON. It is used with adjectives of more than two syllables, and with some adjectives of two syllables.

Positive	Comparative	Superlative
plentiful	more plentiful	most plentiful
beautiful	more beautiful	most beautiful
cautious	less cautious	least cautious
intelligent	more intelligent	most intelligent
patient	more patient	most patient
difficult	less difficult	least difficult

It should be noticed that some adjectives may be compared by regular comparison or by phrasal comparison.

Positive	Comparative	Superlative
simple	simpler	simplest
simple	more simple	most simple

100

3. The third way of forming the comparative and superlative degrees of adjectives is by using different words for different degrees. This is called IRREGULAR COMPARISON.

Positive	Comparative	Superlative
good, well	better	best
bad, evil, ill	worse	worst
far	farther	farthest
many, much	more	most
little	less, lesser	least
fore	former	foremost
near	nearer	nearest (next)
late	later (latter)	latest (last)
old	older (elder)	oldest (eldest)

Notice that the last three adjectives above are regularly compared, but that in addition each has other forms showing irregular comparison.

Note: Some adjectives represent qualities that do not vary. Such adjectives cannot be compared, as:

straight, circular, square, daily, yearly.

EXERCISE 93

Give the comparative and superlative forms of the following adjectives:

gay	kind	good	thick	worthy	healthy
big	near	bad	quiet	careful	pleasant
old	late	small	lucky	lonely	generous
hot	safe	great	little	wealthy	beautiful
far	much	early	pretty	earnest	wonderful
deep	easy	sweet	clever	famous	industrious
dark	thin	pale	high	liberal	majestic
quick	large	poor	rich	sincere	handsome
true	dull	mean	noble	happy	

101

Comparison of Adverbs

Adverbs are compared in the same way as adjectives.

1. By adding *er* and *est* to the positive degree. (regular comparison):

Positive	Comparative	Superlative
fast	faster	fastest
soon	sooner	soonest

2. By the use of *more* and *most* before the positive form (phrasal comparison):

Positive	Comparative	Superlative
swiftly	more swiftly	most swiftly

3. By using different words (irregular comparison):

Positive	Comparative	Superlative
well	better	best
much	more	most
far	farther	farthest
little	less	least
badly	worse	worst

Some adverbs that cannot be compared include the following:

now, then, there, here, too, yonder, very, so, therefore, how.

Correct Usage

The comparative degree is used to show that one person or thing possesses more (or less) of a certain quality than another person or thing. Two colours may be bright, but one may be brighter than the other. We must always use the comparative form when comparing two persons or things. It is wrong to say: This is the *brightest* of the two colours. We must say: This is the *brighter* of the two colours.

The superlative degree is used in comparing more than two persons or things. We must say: John is the *tallest* of the three boys. There are many pupils in our class, but I am the *youngest*.

EXERCISE 94

Write out each sentence, using the correct word in italics.

1. Both drawings are good, but yours is the (*best, better*).
2. Is wood or steel the (*more, most*) durable?
3. This is the (*faster, fastest*) of the two horses.
4. He is the (*less, least*) talkative of all the children.
5. John is the (*tallest, taller*) of the two boys.
6. Both rivers are wide, but this is the (*widest, wider*).
7. This is the (*brighter, brightest*) of the two rooms.
8. Is your father or mother the (*most, more*) musical?
9. This is the (*duller, dullest*) of all the books I have read.
10. He is the (*stronger, strongest*) of the two men.
11. This is the (*busier, busiest*) season of the year for farmers.
12. Which is the (*youngest, younger*) of the two brothers?

CHAPTER XI

SIMPLE AND COMPOUND SENTENCES

Simple and Compound Sentences,
and their Analysis

Simple and Compound Sentences

Study the following groups of sentences:

1. We heard a plane.
   We did not see it.
   We heard a plane, but we did not see it.
2. The boys cleaned the yard.
   The girls planted the flowers.
   The boys cleaned the yard, and the girls planted the flowers.

We see:

(1) In each of the first two sentences of a group there is one subject and one predicate.

(2) The first two sentences of each group are joined to form the third sentence.

A sentence which contains only one subject and one predicate is called a SIMPLE SENTENCE.

A part of a sentence which contains a subject and a predicate is called a CLAUSE. Clauses which can form sentences are called PRINCIPAL CLAUSES. They are also sometimes called INDEPENDENT CLAUSES.

You will notice that in the third sentence of each group above the clauses are the same as the first two sentences of the group. A sentence which is made up of two or more principal clauses is called a COMPOUND SENTENCE. The verb *compound* means *to combine*. Two or more statements are combined to form a compound sentence.

Conjunctions in Compound Sentences

The words most commonly used to connect the clauses of compound sentences are *and* and *but*. You studied these words when they joined words and phrases used in the same way in the sentence, and you learned that they are called CONJUNCTIONS. You now see that conjunctions also join clauses used in the same way in the sentence.

Study these sentences.

1. Parts of Holland are below the sea-level.
2. Great dykes hold back the water.
3. By this means much land is saved for cultivation.
4. Parts of Holland are below the sea-level, but great dykes hold back the water, and by this means much land is saved for cultivation.

Notice that the first three sentences are closely connected in thought. In such cases, it is often desirable to combine several statements into one compound sentence. This has been done in the fourth sentence.

Select the clauses of the fourth sentence. It is evident that the clauses are equal in value, since each can form a sentence. They are therefore principal clauses. Note that we omit the connecting word (conjunction) in reading the clauses.

EXERCISE 95

Combine the following simple sentences into compound sentences.

1. Mary took her umbrella. She did not need it.
2. He called at the house. He left a parcel.
3. Queen Bess smiled. She walked dryshod upon the outspread cloak.
4. I could stand. I was too weak to walk.

5. Coke is a kind of fuel. It is not so heavy as coal.
6. He bought some land. He built a house on it.
7. Dark clouds gathered quickly. It did not rain.
8. He was in a dangerous place. He was not afraid.
9. Our new school was built last year. The formal opening was today.
10. My aunt has been ill for a long time. She never complains.
11. I spent my holidays at a camp. I had a good time.
12. The river is frozen. It is not safe for skating.
13. I searched for my knife. I did not find it.

EXERCISE 96

Divide each compound sentence into simple sentences.

1. The snow fell fast, and a white blanket soon covered the ground.
2. Henry jumped for the ball, but it whizzed past him.
3. We wanted to buy his dog, but he would not sell it.
4. The soil was poor, and little rain fell that year, but the settlers rejoiced at their first crop.
5. The boys bought peanuts, and in the park they fed the saucy squirrels.
6. I raised the window, and a bat flew in.
7. The spring weather was unfavourable, but the summer brought rains, and the crops revived.
8. They did not expect us so soon, and they were not ready to receive us.
9. The thunder rolled, and the lightning flashed, but we ran on.
10. There were fish in the river, but we could not catch them.
11. The outcome of the election was uncertain, and excitement ran high.
12. His father gave him good advice, and he never forgot it.
13. My watch was slow, and I missed the train.
14. There was much snow during the winter, and in the spring the river was high.

Other Conjunctions in Compound Sentences

In addition to *and* and *but*, a few other conjunctions are used to join clauses in compound sentences. These include: *or, nor, so, for, yet.*

Examples: I did not have enough money, *or* I would have bought it.

The problem was difficult, *yet* he solved it easily.

The water in the well is good, *for* it was recently tested.

EXERCISE 97

Select the clauses in these sentences.

1. I tried very hard, and at last I succeeded.
2. They were away, and the house was very still.
3. There were frosty nights last spring, and the apple blossoms were injured.
4. It is noon, for the bell has rung.
5. The sailors threatened to throw Columbus into the sea, but he still refused to turn back.
6. Frank will plant the garden, or he will get someone to do it.
7. Then the brothers were taken to Joseph's house, and they bowed to the earth before him.
8. The boys rented a cabin, and they lived there for a week.
9. We did not see you, or we would have waited.
10. The twilight deepened, and the stars shone out.
11. Cold weather came early, for the ground was frozen in November.
12. Planes circled the wreckage, but few survivors were seen.
13. She is clever, yet she did not pass.
14. We must cultivate the soil, or crops will not grow well.
15. We could not see the plane, nor could we hear it.
16. The power was off, so we did not hear the news.

Missing Subjects

When two principal clauses have the same subject, it is often omitted in the second clause. This makes the sentence read more smoothly.

Example: He petted the horse for a time, and then leaped lightly on its back.

Always supply the missing subject when you select the clauses in a compound sentence, as follows:

He petted the horse for a time — principal clause.
then he leaped lightly on its back — principal clause.

EXERCISE 98

Select the clauses in these sentences.

1. His horse was shot under him, but he mounted another and joined a second charge.
2. We visited from island to island, and traded with great profit.
3. She went to London and was presented at court.
4. Tom Sawyer surveyed the fence, and all gladness left him, and a deep melancholy settled down upon his spirit.
5. We found tracks and traced the animal to its den.
6. This must be fertile soil, for the crops are abundant.
7. The sparrow hopped up to him and looked at him for a moment, with her head on one side.
8. A soft answer turneth away wrath, but grievous words stir up anger.
9. He arrived home early and went directly to his room.
10. The sun came from behind a cloud and flooded the valley with light.
11. I hunted everywhere for the lost kitten, but could not find it.
12. We listened intently and peered into the darkness, but we could not hear or see anything.

Graphic Analysis of Compound Sentences

In analysing compound sentences, omit the conjunctions, and analyse each principal clause.

Example: We landed (on the island,) and [the] boys pitched our tent (in an open field.)

Conjunctions are sometimes omitted in compound sentences. This is particularly true in poetry, but is also found in prose, especially where there are three or more principal clauses in the sentence.

Examples: [The] chateau burned; [the] [nearest] trees shrivelled; trees [at a distance] surrounded the burning building (with a new forest of smoke.)

(There) lies [the] port; [the] vessel puffs her sail;

(There) gloom [the] [dark] [broad] seas.

EXERCISE 99

Write each sentence and analyse the clauses graphically. If you have any difficulty with this exercise, you should review the section on *Aids in Analysis*. (See page 10.)

1. The ragged stranger wiped his feet carefully on the mat, and he removed his hat politely.

2. There he opened a shop for his father, but business was not good.

3. Along the line of smoky hills
   The crimson forest stands,
   And all the day the blue-jay calls
   Throughout the autumn lands.

4. In our country we reckon a man's wealth in money and lands, but in Lapland wealth is reckoned in reindeer.
5. Great mountains tower above its shore,
   Green rushes fringe its brim,
   And o'er its breast for evermore
   The wanton breezes skim.
6. The merchants gathered stones and threw them at the apes in the trees.
7. In his youth he formed the habit of reading widely, and now he derives great pleasure from it.
8. Snow and ice cover the peak of the mountain during the whole year, but the lower slope is bare in the summer.
9. Edison was a great inventor, and his discoveries have helped us all.
10. For me spring is the best time of the year, but many people prefer the fall.
11. The stove in the old school was large, and it easily heated the room.
12. British Columbia has developed many industries, but it still holds the glamour of its pioneer days.

CHAPTER XII

COMPLEX SENTENCES

Subordinate Clauses, Complex Sentences, Clausal Analysis,
Compound-Complex Sentences

Subordinate Clauses

Study the following pairs of sentences:

1. I came *then.*
   I came *when you called me.*
2. We looked *there.*
   We looked *where he pointed.*
3. This is a *treasured* book.
   This is a book *which I treasure.*
4. That was a *suitable* time.
   That was a time *which was suitable.*

An examination of all the parts in italics shows:
(1) In the second sentence of each of the first two pairs of sentences a group of words takes the place of an adverb.
(2) In the second sentence of each of the third and fourth pairs of sentences a group of words takes the place of an adjective.

These groups are:

> *when you called me*
> *where he pointed*
> *which I treasure*
> *which was suitable*

You can see that each group has a subject and a predicate. Each group is therefore a clause. It is evident that no group expresses a complete thought, because each depends on some other part of its sentence to make its meaning clear. Such a group of words is called a SUBORDINATE CLAUSE.

111

In this exercise the subordinate clauses are in italics.

(a) Select the subject and predicate of each subordinate clause.

1. We waited *until the train left.*
2. Men *who are honest* are respected.
3. He has work *that exercises his mind.*
4. I will go *unless I am too tired.*
5. We went to the store *after you left us.*
6. A forest once grew *where this city stands.*
7. I worked during the holidays *because I needed the money.*
8. They will play in the game *if they are needed.*
9. I have not seen him *since he left school.*
10. The deer ran into the woods *as we approached.*
11. My father has some coins *that are very old.*
12. This is the place *where we live.*
13. I went to school *though I did not feel well.*
14. Do you remember the times *when we played together?*
15. The miller ground the grain *while the farmer waited.*
16. We reached home *before the storm began.*

(b) State whether each subordinate clause has the value of an adverb or an adjective.

1. The trees *that grow there* are small.
2. I drove carefully *because the road was icy.*
3. The man *who sent you* is my friend.
4. I shall see you *when you return.*
5. The apples *which you sent* were delicious.
6. I left the house *before he arrived.*
7. My dog goes *where I go.*
8. That is an insect *which injures flowers.*
9. The owner was away *when the house burned.*
10. We bought the house *which your father built.*
11. He read a book *while he waited.*
12. My father knows the artist *whom you met.*

Adverb and Adjective Clauses

A subordinate clause which has the value of an adverb is called an ADVERB CLAUSE. A subordinate clause which has the value of an adjective is called an ADJECTIVE CLAUSE.

A word, phrase, or subordinate clause can sometimes be used to express the same idea.

Examples: 1. He is an *honourable* man.   (adjective)
He is a man *of honour*.   (adjective phrase)
He is a man *who is honourable*.
(adjective clause)
2. I went *early*.   (adverb)
I went *at an early hour*.   (adverb phrase)
I went *while it was early*.   (adverb clause)

EXERCISE 101

Write each sentence, using a subordinate clause in place of the word or phrase in italics.

1. I remained at home *for that reason*.
2. Iron always expands *then*.
3. That was the farm *of my grandfather*.
4. He is the *guilty* man.
5. People *with good manners* avoid embarrassing others.
6. We sat under a *shady* tree.
7. I left *at sunrise*.
8. He lived in Australia *during his youth*.
9. *Valuable* papers are generally kept in vaults.
10. These are *noticeable* symptoms.
11. He is a *sincere* man.
12. That is a matter *for consideration*.
13. They live *at the fork in the road*.
14. *Contagious* diseases should be controlled.
15. They are *respectable* people.
16. I went *at his request*.

113

Relation of Clauses

We give the relation of adverb and adjective clauses as follows:

Examples: He sometimes reads while he eats.

The hat that you selected suits me.

while he eats — a subordinate adverb clause modifying the verb *reads*.

that you selected — a subordinate adjective clause modifying the noun *hat*.

Write each subordinate clause, and give its kind and relation.

1. I chose this book because our teacher recommended it.
2. The men rested while it was raining.
3. The flowers that you gathered are fragrant.
4. You have opportunities now which will never come again.
5. We like people who are polite.
6. They fish where the water is not deep.
7. He remained until the work was finished.
8. The girl that you met is my cousin.
9. They left here as the sun was setting.
10. I will tell him when he comes.
11. Do you know the piece that the band is playing?
12. I laughed when I heard the joke.
13. When Alice in Wonderland ate the cake, she grew extremely tall.
14. The pupils went in before the bell rang.
15. He is the man who bought the house.
16. While he was speaking we were called from the room.
17. Peaches fall when they are very ripe.
18. When the day dawned we were far on our journey.
19. I always do some work before I leave for school.
20. He returned the money which he found.

Complex Sentences

Examine these sentences. You will see that each of the first two sentences contains a principal clause and a subordinate clause. The third sentence contains a principal clause and two subordinate clauses.

1. The mercury in a thermometer contracts when the weather is cold.
2. Many people live in houses that their ancestors built.
3. As he was putting the cup to his lips, he noticed a dying soldier who cast eager eyes upon it.

A sentence which contains a principal clause and one or more subordinate clauses is called a COMPLEX SENTENCE.

Clausal Analysis

When we select all the clauses in a sentence and tell the kind and the relation of each subordinate clause, we are doing CLAUSAL ANALYSIS. Here is the clausal analysis of the third sentence of the group above.

he noticed a dying soldier — principal clause.

As he was putting the cup to his lips — a subordinate adverb clause modifying the verb *noticed.*

who cast eager eyes upon it — a subordinate adjective clause modifying the noun *soldier.*

EXERCISE 103

Using the work shown above as a model, give in writing the clausal analysis of each sentence.

1. We remained in the cabin while the storm lasted.
2. That was a time which I shall never forget.
3. The man who built this house was a good carpenter.
4. When the winter is nearly over the maple sap will start to run.
5. As we neared home our hearts beat happily.

6. After we had latched the gate we hurried to the house because we were cold and wet.
7. I know a place where blackberries grow.
8. When the news of Cabot's achievement spread in Bristol he became a popular hero.
9. He has many friends because he is friendly.
10. When the ice melts in the spring the logs that have been prepared during the winter are floated down the river.

EXERCISE 104

Decide on the clausal analysis of each sentence, and then give the work orally in class.

1. Before school closes we make plans for our holidays.
2. An incubator is a machine which requires daily attention.
3. A great plain where sheep now roam was once the site of a city.
4. Men who sought the Northwest passage were bold and daring.
5. When you study you make good use of time that will never return.
6. He wore a panama hat that had seen many summers.
7. Basketball is a game which I enjoy very much.
8. If you learn to be observant you will see many things that most people miss.
9. Our dog howls when I play the harmonica.
10. After we have had enough practice, the coach will select the boys who will play on the team.
11. I did not sleep well because I was excited over the game.
12. After we ate our lunch, we went to see an old man whom we had met when we were there before.

EXERCISE 105

Decide on the clausal analysis of each sentence, and then give the work orally in class.

1. I know the song that the bluebird is singing.

116

2. While I am lying on the grass
   Thy twofold shout I hear.
3. He lifted the book which I had laid on the floor.
4. My heart leaps up when I behold
   A rainbow in the sky.
5. When snow and ice cover the ground the Laplander travels in his sled.
6. Poor Gulliver was constantly exposed to all sorts of dangers because he was so small.
7. As he went along by the canal he admired the flowers which grew there.
8. Ants that do not build in the soil sometimes gather a variety of material from the neighbourhood of the place that has been chosen for a nest.
9. The redbreast sings from the tall larch
   That stands beside my door.
10. Between the dark and the daylight,
    When the night is beginning to lower,
    Comes a pause in the day's occupations,
    That is known as the children's hour.
11. Before he had finished at school, he began work in the newspaper office which he now owns.
12. When he goes for a walk, his friend is always with him.
13. The dog stayed where his master left him.
14. His father owns the largest farm that is in the county.
15. She talked constantly while she sewed.
16. The fishermen wore boots that reached to their knees.
17. The ship will not sail if the weather is unfavourable.
18. As I was going to school one morning, a squirrel ran into its hole in the path where I was walking.
19. While he was walking along the beach, the keen eyes of the old sailor saw a ship that was floundering in the heavy sea.
20. The general was buried with all the honours which his country could give him.

Noun Clauses

Analyse the first sentence of each of the following pairs, and select the clauses in the second sentence of each pair.

1. We heard your reply.
   We heard what you said.

2. I know the man.
   I know who he is.

3. They realized the danger.
   They realized that there was danger.

In each pair, notice the similarity between the object in the first sentence and the subordinate clause in the second sentence.

We may state our observation and conclusion in this way:

(1) In the second sentence of each pair a clause replaces a noun which is the object of the verb in the first sentence.

(2) Therefore the clause in the second sentence of each pair has the value of a noun, and is used as the object of a verb.

A clause which has the value of a noun is called a NOUN CLAUSE.

EXERCISE 106

Select the noun clauses in these sentences.

1. I think that I shall ride.
2. Do you remember where you put the bat?
3. I understand that he speaks several languages.
4. My father knew where we were.
5. Perhaps you can recall what he told you.
6. The jury decided that he was innocent.
7. The boys believed that they were on the right road.
8. Have you decided where you will hang the picture?
9. He said that we might go.
10. I have not heard why he gave up his position.

Noun Clauses as Subjects

You have learned that a noun clause may be used as the object of a verb. A study of the following sentences will show you that the noun clause may also be used as the subject of a verb. Select the noun clause in the second sentence of each of the following pairs:

1. It is true.
   What you say is true.

2. His failure is hard to understand.
   That he failed is hard to understand.

3. That is a secret.
   Where it is hidden is a secret.

4. The time is not known.
   When it happened is not known.

5. It is here.
   What I found is here.

If you ask questions as you were taught in the section *Aids in Analysis,* on page 10, it will help you to select noun clauses used as subjects or objects in sentences. It is interesting to note that a noun clause is sometimes introduced by *when* and *where,* which often introduce adverb clauses. A noun clause may also be introduced by *that,* which often introduces adjective clauses.

Relation of Noun Clauses

We give the relation of a noun clause as follows:

Examples: I heard that you won the prize.
　　　　　What you say interests me.

that you won the prize — a noun clause, object of the verb *heard.*

what you say — a noun clause, subject of the verb *interests.*

Write each noun clause and give its relation.

1. The boy discovered that he was alone in the building.
2. Where he got his money is a mystery.
3. I observed that his fingers were very long.
4. What he said amused her.
5. Always remember that honesty is the best policy.
6. The Greeks saw that they must gain their end by craft.
7. He gave away what he had saved.
8. I noticed that his clothes were carefully brushed.
9. We thought that we would never reach home.
10. Where he went I did not ask.
11. When an earthquake will occur is never known.
12. We admire what you did.
13. Columbus believed that the earth was round.
14. I did not hear what you said.
15. We did not know that you were a musician.

Give orally in class each noun clause and its relation.

1. We saw that the lake was too rough for pleasant sailing.
2. I never could understand why you did that.
3. Bees know where the clover is.
4. That he plays baseball well is true.
5. The sailor knows when the wind will change.
6. What you tell us is interesting.
7. My brother promised that he would send me a present.
8. She does not know that I am here.
9. Never say what you do not mean.
10. I realized that you would be pleased.
11. I dreamt that I passed my examination.
12. We sometimes forget that others have feelings.
13. When good fortune will come cannot be foreseen.
14. You have described what happened very well.

Separation of Clauses

When a subordinate clause modifies a word in another subordinate clause, list the clauses separately.

Examples: We did not know the way when we reached the place where the road divided.

I discovered where there is a beach that is excellent for bathing.

The clauses in the first sentence are:

We did not know the way — principal clause.
when we reached the place — a subordinate adverb clause modifying the verb *did know*.
where the road divided — a subordinate adjective clause modifying the noun *place*.

The clauses in the second sentence are:

I discovered — principal clause.

where there is a beach — a subordinate noun clause, object of the verb *discovered*.

that is excellent for bathing — a subordinate adjective clause modifying the noun *beach*.

Please notice that in the second example the principal clause *I discovered* does not include the object of the verb, which, strictly speaking, it should do. In clausal analysis it is simpler to separate the principal clause from the noun clause which is an object.

However, when a noun clause is used as a subject it must be included in the principal clause.

Example: Where he went is a mystery.

The clauses in this sentence are:

Where he went is a mystery — principal clause.
Where he went — a noun clause, subject of the verb *is*.

121

Give in writing the clausal analysis of each sentence. Include the principal clause, and give the kind and the relation of each subordinate clause.

1. The boy searched for the money which he had lost.
2. What I shall do then I do not know.
3. When my pony died I felt that I had lost a friend.
4. One never knows what he can do until he tries.
5. Unless you go with me I will not go.
6. A wise man is one who never tells all that he knows.
7. When I was a child I often wondered what held the earth in place.
8. Although he had a golden crown he was not satisfied.
9. After we reached home I realized that I was very tired.
10. I know people who always sing when they are happy.

Decide on the clausal analysis of each sentence, and then give the work orally in class.

1. The jacket that you want is expensive.
2. When I was on my way to school I met a man who had an axe on his shoulder.
3. He said that I was a fine little fellow.
4. Because this pleased me I said that I would turn the grindstone for him.
5. When the evidence has all been given you will agree that my dog did not kill the sheep.
6. The man who tries to profit by his mistakes is wise.
7. If you consider my offer carefully you will find that I have been generous.
8. That is the reason which he gave when he left.
9. An old man whom I knew when I was young told me that he had once talked with Queen Victoria.
10. When I went to the store I forgot what I was told to buy.

Decide on the clausal analysis of each sentence, and then give the work orally in class.

1. I thought that perhaps Shakespeare had stayed at the inn where we slept.
2. If you know where he is you should tell us.
3. What I thought then is still my opinion.
4. When he saw that they had brought his brother Benjamin, he was very much pleased.
5. That you were right I have never doubted.
6. The caravan drivers from whom he bought spices told him that they came from a great distance.
7. I have not forgotten many amusing things that happened when I was a child.
8. I remember how the pony stopped of his own accord when we met anyone on the road.
9. If he had known before he sold the farm that there was oil on it, he would have asked a higher price.

Compound-Complex Sentences

Examine this sentence, and you will see that it contains two principal clauses and one subordinate clause.

The youth walked with a light and joyous step, and he sang a merry song as he hurried on.

You see that the clauses are:

The youth walked with a light and joyous step — principal clause.
he sang a merry song — principal clause.
as he hurried on — a subordinate adverb clause modifying the verb *sang*.

A sentence that contains two or more principal clauses and one or more subordinate clauses is called a COMPOUND-COMPLEX SENTENCE.

Decide on the clausal analysis of each sentence, and then give the work orally in class.

1. He asked why you were absent, and I replied that I did not know.

2. We tapped the trees early, but the sap did not run well because the weather was too mild.

3. He says that I should study medicine because doctors do so much good, but I know what I want to do.

4. When we left for camp we expected that our supplies would be there, and we were greatly disappointed when we discovered that they had not arrived.

5. There is a park near Orillia which is a notable spot because Champlain camped there when he was on his way to Lake Huron, and in the park now stands a monument that was erected in memory of the great explorer.

6. I know that you have given me good advice, and I promise that I will not disappoint you.

7. He said that every man is the master of his own fate, but I think we must admit that chance does play a part.

8. Sunset is fading beyond the hills and the shades of evening steal softly into the valley where our tent is pitched.

9. When our team came out on the ice they knew that they would have to work hard, and during the game every player used all the strength and skill that he had.

10. That he was a great man can not be denied, but I recall that he had a long line of distinguished ancestors from whom he inherited much.

CHAPTER XIII

CLASSES OF CONJUNCTIONS
Co-ordinate, Correlative, Subordinate, Phrasal

Co-ordinate Conjunctions

You have learned that certain conjunctions join words and phrases used in the same way in a sentence. They are also used to join principal clauses in a compound sentence. Study carefully the use of each conjunction in these sentences.

Examples: 1. Ice *and* snow covered the pond.
2. He worked early *and* late.
3. The blankets were light *but* warm.
4. We sat *and* talked for an hour.
5. I will work in the factory *or* in the office.
6. There was a fire, *for* the bell rang.

Certain conjunctions are also used to join subordinate clauses of the same kind and use.

Examples: 1. He knows what makes clouds *and* why they cross the sky.
2. He studies before he goes to school *and* while his mind is fresh.
3. Those were times when money was scarce *and* when people worked long hours.

Conjunctions which join words, phrases, and clauses used in the same way in a sentence are called CO-ORDINATE CONJUNCTIONS. Co-ordinate means *of the same rank*; the joined parts have the same rank or grammatical value.

The most commonly used co-ordinate conjunctions are: *and, but, or, for, yet, nor, so.*

(a) Use each of the co-ordinate conjunctions listed on page 125 in a sentence to join two principal clauses.

(b) Use any two words in the list in a compound sentence which contains three clauses.

(c) Use the word *and* in sentences to join:

two nouns	two adverbs	two noun clauses
two verbs	two adjective phrases	two adjective clauses
two adjectives	two adverb phrases	two adverb clauses

Correlative Conjunctions

Co-ordinate conjunctions which are used in pairs are called CORRELATIVE CONJUNCTIONS.

Examples: He locked *both* the doors *and* the windows.

Either you *or* I should do the shopping.

Neither the man *nor* the boy could swim.

The most commonly used correlative conjunctions are: *either-or; neither-nor; both-and; not only-but also.* Notice that each pair forms a single conjunction.

Subordinate Conjunctions

Study the italicized words in the following sentences:

1. We waited *until* the train came.
2. This is the town *where* he lives.
3. I know *that* my answer is correct.

You will notice:

(1) Each word in italics begins a subordinate clause.

(2) Each word in italics joins the subordinate clause to some other word in the sentence.

A word that introduces a subordinate clause, and joins it to some other word in the sentence, is called a SUBORDINATE CONJUNCTION. Please note that a subordinate conjunction is considered a necessary part of the subordinate clause, and must be included in it.

The most commonly used subordinate conjunctions are: *after, although, as, because, before, for* (meaning *because*), *if, since, than, though, unless, until, when, where, while.*

In this list of subordinate conjunctions, you will notice a number of words that you have already seen used as prepositions. It is not difficult to tell whether a word is used as a preposition or a subordinate conjunction in a sentence, since the subordinate conjunction always introduces a clause containing a subject and predicate.

Note that the word *than* is a subordinate conjunction. It usually introduces a subordinate clause which is not complete.

Examples: I am older *than* you. He walks faster *than* I.

The complete sentences are:

I am older *than* you are. He walks faster *than* I walk.

The subordinate clause in the first sentence modifies the adjective *older.* The subordinate clause in the second sentence modifies the adverb *faster.*

EXERCISE 114

(a) Write complex sentences, using each of the conjunctions listed above to introduce a subordinate clause. (b) Write five complex sentences with three clauses in each, using any two of these conjunctions in each sentence.

Phrasal Conjunctions

Some conjunctions consist of two or more words, and are called PHRASAL CONJUNCTIONS.

Examples: We shall leave *as soon as* he comes.
He walks *as if* he is tired.
The boys *as well as* the girls are sleepy.

127

In the preceding sentences, *as soon as* and *as if* are SUBORDINATE PHRASAL CONJUNCTIONS. In the third sentence, *as well as* is a CO-ORDINATE PHRASAL CONJUNCTION.

Other subordinate phrasal conjunctions commonly used are: *provided that, in order that, so that, as though.*

Uses of Conjunctions

We give the uses of conjunctions which join clauses as follows:

Examples: When the fishermen landed to dry their nets, they met some Indians, and they began to trade in furs.

when — a subordinate conjunction introducing the subordinate clause *when the fishermen landed to dry their nets*, and joining the clause to the verb *met.*

and — a co-ordinate conjunction joining the principal clauses *they met some Indians* and *they began to trade in furs.*

EXERCISE 115

Give in writing the use of each conjunction.

1. He plucked a rose from the bush, and the rose became in his hand a beautiful golden flower.
2. When he had been on the island ten or twelve days he realized that he would lose count of the time if he did not find some way of measuring it.
3. We soon reached the level country and drove for many miles over a beautiful plain that I had never seen before.
4. I enjoy a walk on a cold winter night when the snow crunches beneath my feet and when the stars sparkle overhead.
5. The firemen came when they were called, but it was too late.
6. When night comes, the land loses its heat very quickly because it has not stored it up, and the land air grows cold.

128

Give orally the use of each conjunction, and the relation of the joined parts. (See page 25.)

1. Do you use tea or coffee?
2. We waited and watched for an hour.
3. He is a kindly and generous fellow.
4. The can bobbed up and down on the waves.
5. He had neither money nor position.
6. The sun shines on friend and foe alike.
7. Boys and girls work together in the garden.
8. The woman is poor but contented.
9. She types slowly but accurately.
10. You are either clever or lucky.
11. The weather was neither cold nor hot.
12. Smoke and steam were escaping through the doors and through the windows.

Give orally the use of each conjunction.

1. When he realized what had happened he was jubilant.
2. We arrived at the camp after darkness had fallen, and when day dawned we looked upon a sight which surpassed in beauty anything that we had ever seen.
3. Because the roads were bad we left early for school, but the bell had rung before we arrived.
4. When you consult your dictionary for the meaning of a word, you may see that it is defined by several synonyms as well as by one or more definitions.
5. We soon passed your island, and I recognized the very spot where we camped last summer.
6. When I felt a tug on my line I thought that I had caught a large fish.

CHAPTER XIV

CONJUNCTIVE PRONOUNS

Conjunctive Pronouns and their Antecedents

Conjunctive Pronouns

Examine these pairs of sentences.

1. John is the boy. He did it.
   John is the boy *who* did it.
2. These are problems. We must solve them.
   These are problems *which* we must solve.

In these pairs of sentences we see:

(1) Two simple sentences are joined to form a complex sentence.

(2) In the first pair, the word *who* joins the two simple sentences, and also replaces the pronoun *he*. Therefore *who* is both a conjunction and a pronoun.

(3) In the second pair, the word *which* joins the two simple sentences, and also replaces the pronoun *them*. Therefore *which* is both a conjunction and a pronoun.

A word that has the value of both a conjunction and a pronoun is called a CONJUNCTIVE PRONOUN. It is also sometimes called a RELATIVE PRONOUN.

In the second sentence of the first pair, the words *boy* and *who* represent the same person. It is easy to see that *who* refers to the noun *boy*. In the second sentence of the second pair, the word *which* refers to the noun *problems*. The word to which a conjunctive pronoun refers is called its ANTECEDENT. The word antecedent means *going before*.

A conjunctive pronoun and its antecedent are

130

always in different clauses. A conjunctive pronoun has the same person and number as its antecedent, but its case is determined by its use in its own clause.

Examples: John is the boy *who* did it.

These are problems *which* we must solve.

In the first sentence, *who* is third person, singular number, because its antecedent *boy* is third person, singular number. However, notice that *who* is in the nominative case because it is subject of the verb *did* in its own clause. In the second sentence, *which* is third person, plural number, because its antecedent *problems* is third person, plural number. It is in the objective case because it is object of the verb *must solve* in its own clause.

Examine these sentences:

1. He related *what* had happened.
2. *What* you say is true.
3. I know *what* you mean.
4. I asked *what* he was thinking about.

By selecting the clauses in each sentence, and by studying the word *what*, we see that in each sentence *what* is a conjunctive pronoun. *What* is an unusual conjunctive pronoun because it has no antecedent. It really stands for the words *that which*, and might be said to contain its own antecedent. Try substituting the words *that which* for *what* in each of the above sentences.

Like other conjunctive pronouns, *what* takes its case from its own clause. Decide on the case of *what* in each of the above sentences.

The common conjunctive pronouns are: *who, whose, whom, which, that, what.*

131

Case and Relation of Conjunctive Pronouns

The case and relation of conjunctive pronouns should be given as follows:

Examples: She is the girl *that* sang so well.
There is a man *whom* I know.
The teacher praised the pupils, *whose* desks were tidy.
He remembered *what* happened.

that — a conjunctive pronoun, third person singular, nominative case, subject of the verb *sang*.

whom — a conjunctive pronoun, third person singular, objective case, object of the verb *know*.

whose — a conjunctive pronoun, third person plural, possessive case, showing the possession of *desks*.

what — a conjunctive pronoun, third person singular, nominative case, subject of the verb *happened*.

EXERCISE 118

Give in writing the person, number, case, and relation of each conjunctive pronoun.

1. These are the new books which I bought.
2. He repeated what he had heard.
3. The people whom I live with are very kind.
4. He is the man that directed the orchestra.
5. They are the people whose car was damaged.
6. We know what you think about it.
7. Here is a boy who will guide you.
8. That is the hat which I want.
9. He listened to what you said.
10. This is the house that Jack built.
11. I recall the man whom you mention.
12. Is she the girl whom you skated with?
13. These are scenes which delight me.
14. I know he is a boy that you can trust.

Care with Conjunctive Pronouns

Many errors in speech and writing are made in using the words *who, whose,* and *whom.* Notice that:

(1) *Who, whose,* and *whom* are three forms of the same pronoun. Always use *who* in the nominative case, *whose* in the possessive case, and *whom* in the objective case.

(2) The conjunctive pronoun *whom* may be the object of a verb or a preposition in its own clause.

Examples: Did you recognize the man *whom* we passed?
He is the stranger *whom* I spoke of.

As you see in the second example, it is correct to separate a conjunctive pronoun from the preposition which takes it as its object. This sentence can also be written: He is the stranger of *whom* I spoke.

(3) Never use *which* in referring to persons. It is used only in referring to things.

(4) *That* is used in referring to either persons or things.

(5) *Whose* is usually used in referring to persons. However, it is also correct to use it to replace *of which* in regard to things.

Examples: I returned the picture, the frame *of which* was broken.
I returned the picture *whose* frame was broken.

EXERCISE 119

Write out each sentence, using the proper word in brackets. Be prepared to give the reason for your choice.

1. Did you notice the girls (*who, whom*) went in ahead of us?
2. Is he the friend of (*whom, who*) you spoke?
3. He is the man (*that, which*) did it.
4. Are they the relatives (*who, whom*) you visited?
5. These are natives (*who, whom*) never harm strangers.

6. Anyone (*who, whom*) you choose may go with us.
7. It was the boys (*who, whom*) were noisy.
8. I do not know the girls (*who, whom*) we passed.
9. He is a man (*who, whom*) is always helping others.
10. The people (*who, which*) made these brooms are blind.
11. We recognized the man (*who, whom*) had given us a ride.
12. He is a mechanic (*whom, who*) my father works with.
13. He is the boy (*who, whom*) should do it.
14. They are people (*who, whom*) we know well.
15. He is a man for (*whom, who*) I have great respect.

CHAPTER XV

VERBALS

Verbals: Participles, Gerunds, Infinitives

Participles

Let us examine the words in italics in the following sentences:

1. The boy *throws* the ball.
2. The boy *throwing* the ball is my brother.

In the first sentence, the action verb *throws* takes the object *ball*. In the second sentence, the action word *throwing* takes the object *ball*, and is therefore like a verb. It is also like an adjective, since it describes the noun *boy*. A word that has the value of a verb and an adjective is called a VERBAL ADJECTIVE or PARTICIPLE.

Study the words in italics in these sentences.

1. The man *walking* along the road is a farmer.
2. The man *walking* is a farmer.

In the first sentence, *walking* has the value of a verb, since it is an action word and has an adverbial modifier. It also has the value of an adjective, since it modifies the noun *man*. In the second sentence, *walking* has the value of a verb, since it is an action word and may have an adverbial modifier. It is an adjective, since it modifies the noun *man*. Therefore *walking* is used in both sentences as a participle.

Read carefully the following sentences, and explain why each word in italics is a participle:

1. The girls *wearing* Irish costumes are in the play.
2. The man *waving* his hand is the referee.

3. The boys *playing* marbles are brothers.
4. Icebergs *drifting* at sea are dangerous.
5. The girls *standing* there attend our school.
6. Weeds *growing* in the garden spoiled its appearance.
7. The dog *barking* is mine.
8. The girl *singing* is an actress.

The participles you have studied have these characteristics:

(a) They end in *ing*.
(b) They are formed from verbs and express action.
(c) They always modify a noun or pronoun.
(d) They may have an object and an adverbial modifier, or they may be without either.

Use and Relation of Participles

The use and relation of a participle should be given as follows:

Examples: We saw children *gathering* flowers.
The people *living* near us are good neighbours.

gathering — a participle. As a verb, it takes the object *flowers*; as an adjective, it modifies the noun *children*.

living — a participle. As a verb, it has the adverbial modifier *near us*; as an adjective, it modifies the noun *people*.

EXERCISE 120(a)

Give in writing the use and the relation of each participle.

1. Children going to school discovered the fire.
2. The men counting the ballots are scrutineers.
3. He watched another boy making a kite.
4. The pupils singing are the oldest in the school.
5. I like to hear clocks ticking.
6. The month just ending was a busy one for me.
7. We found him working among his flowers.
8. The boy eating the apple is my brother.

Give orally the use and the relation of each participle.

1. The tulips opening now were planted last fall.
2. We saw men, women, and children picking tomatoes for the cannery.
3. The man speaking to her is a member of the legislature.
4. A storm coming up suddenly made us hurry home.
5. We passed a canoe drifting in the lake.
6. The man tuning the piano is a good musician.
7. I saw them entering the hall.
8. Wolves howling at night frightened us.
9. We found the child wandering in the park.
10. Saws buzzing made a cheerful noise.
11. People leaving on this plane will be in England tomorrow.
12. Men hunting deer discovered the lake.

Present Participles

All the participles you have studied end in *ing*, and refer to an action that is still going on, which might be called an incomplete action. Read some of the sentences again, noticing particularly the time of the action.

A participle which indicates an incomplete action is called a PRESENT PARTICIPLE.

Past Participles

Study the words in italics in these sentences.

1. We found it *hidden* in a book.
2. A letter *opened* by mistake came in today's mail.
3. The parcel *left* in the car is mine.
4. I like music *played* softly.
5. A tree *fallen* across the road blocked the traffic.
6. A fire *started* by campers did much damage.
7. He is a man *known* for his generosity.
8. They left him *wounded*.

From our study of these sentences, we see:

(a) Each word in italics is formed from a verb and expresses action.

(b) The action is completed. It refers to past time.

(c) Each word in italics modifies a noun or pronoun.

(d) Some words in italics have adverbial modifiers, and some have not.

Since all the words in italics are formed from verbs and express action, and are used as adjectives to modify nouns or pronouns, they must be participles. A participle which indicates a completed action is called a PAST PARTICIPLE.

As you have learned, present participles always end in *ing*. Past participles usually end in *d*, *ed*, *t*, *n*, or *en*.

Note that past participles may have adverbial modifiers, but they never take an object.

Note: You learned earlier that the past participle is used with the auxiliary *have* to form perfect tenses of the verb. It is the third in the list of the principal parts of a verb, as: give, gave, *given*.

Use and Relation of Past Participles

The use and relation of a past participle should be given as follows:

Examples: We saw walls *covered* with ivy.

Many of the people *invited* did not come.

covered — a past participle. As a verb, it has the adverbial modifier *with ivy*; as an adjective, it modifies the noun *walls*.

invited — a past participle. As a verb, it may have an adverbial modifier; as an adjective, it modifies the noun *people*.

Give in writing the use and the relation of each participle, stating whether it is a present or a past participle.

1. The birds ate the grain scattered on the snow.
2. The man, questioned closely, admitted his mistake.
3. The boys fishing by the bridge are having good luck.
4. Supplies dropped from a plane saved many lives.
5. I saw the girls sliding down the hill.
6. Grain sown in good soil usually grows well.
7. The squirrels have food stored away for winter.
8. The chimes ringing from our church are heard in all parts of the town.
9. Words spoken thoughtlessly often cause pain.
10. The peaches, piled in heaps on the ground, soon spoiled.
11. People living on farms are usually busy.
12. We saw trees uprooted by the hurricane.

Give orally the use and the relation of each participle, stating whether it is a present or a past participle.

1. Boys playing along the shore found the damaged canoe.
2. The road begun in the late fall was never finished.
3. Wood chopped in the winter is dried in the summer.
4. We saw several cars almost buried in snow.
5. He caught a fox stealing his chickens.
6. I prize a book given to me by my mother.
7. We passed a blind man using a white cane.
8. They saw us eating dinner in the restaurant.
9. Campers sometimes leave food and papers scattered about.
10. Old people often remember poetry memorized in childhood.
11. Children eating their lunch sat on the steps of the school.
12. King Philip watched his son controlling the horse.

Position of Participles

A participle often comes before the noun or pronoun it modifies. Study the participles in these sentences.

1. *Sleeping* soundly, I did not hear the noisy fire-alarm bell.
2. *Opening* the door, I saw an old man.
3. *Seen* from a plane, objects on the ground look extremely small.
4. *Given* plenty of time, he solved the problem.
5. *Dressed* warmly, we did not feel the cold.

Present Perfect Participles

Study the italicized words in these sentences.

1. *Having locked* the doors, we went to bed quickly in the old cabin.
2. *Having done* their best, the boys did not worry about losing the game.
3. *Having gone* early, we got a good seat very close to the platform.
4. *Having seen* all the sights at the Exhibition, we came home.
5. *Having been absent*, I missed the lesson in my best subject.

Notice that in each sentence the word *having* is used with the past participle of a verb to modify a noun or pronoun. Both words together form the PRESENT PERFECT PARTICIPLE, and in the examples above take an object or adverbial modifier. (You will recall that *have* together with the past participle of the principal verb forms the perfect tenses; here *having* with the past participle of the principal verb forms the present perfect participle.)

Use and Relation of Present Perfect Participle

The use and relation of a present perfect participle should be given as follows:

Example: Having wasted his money, he was penniless.

> *having wasted* — a present perfect participle. As a verb, it takes the object *money*; as an adjective, it modifies the pronoun *he*.

EXERCISE 123

Give orally the use and relation of each participle.

1. The carpenter, having finished his work, went home.
2. Having found a good book, I sat up late to read.
3. Never having travelled by plane, we were eager to start.
4. Encouraged by the cheering, we did our best.
5. The boys, having earned some money, planned ways of spending it.
6. Attacked by bandits, the travellers defended themselves.
7. Bowing to the audience, the pianist left the stage.
8. Having noticed signs of a storm, the hunters returned.
9. Having thanked our host, we hurried away.
10. Laying down his paper, he joined in the conversation.

Participial Phrases

A participle is usually followed by a modifier or an object. The whole group is called a PARTICIPIAL PHRASE. It always has the value of an adjective.

Examples: *Coming in late,* I tried to be very quiet.

> The boy *tending goal* is our new player.
>
> The girl *arranging the hats* is a milliner.
>
> The land *drained by the Saskatchewan River* covers a large part of Western Canada.
>
> My father, *remembering my birthday,* brought me a present.
>
> The gardener, *fearing a frost,* covered his plants.

141

From the preceding examples you can learn how to punctuate sentences that contain participial phrases. The rules are:

(1) A participial phrase at the beginning of a sentence is always followed by a comma.

(2) A participial phrase that merely *describes* is preceded and followed by a comma. We say that it is a non-essential phrase. That is, it may be omitted without seriously changing the meaning of the sentence. The last two examples illustrate this rule.

(3) A participial phrase that points out a particular person or thing is not preceded or followed by a comma. You see this in the second, third, and fourth examples. In such cases, the phrase is an essential or necessary part of the sentence, explaining the word it modifies. It we left out the phrase, the sentence would not convey the complete idea of the writer.

EXERCISE 124

Copy the following sentences, putting in the necessary commas:

1. The soldiers fearing an attack kept a close watch all night.
2. The boy skating in front is the captain of the team.
3. Hampered by head winds the plane was many hours late.
4. The campers knowing the risks of forest fires were very careful.
5. Being aware of danger he was cautious.
6. The man collecting tickets is the conductor.
7. The hunters having built a fire to frighten away wolves rolled up in their blankets.
8. Turning the corner quickly I collided with my friend.
9. Dogs properly trained display much intelligence.
10. The athlete seeming exhausted sank to the ground.
11. That runner making a final effort won the race.

Gerunds

Study the words in italics in these sentences.

1. We *read* books.
2. *Reading* books in the library is a pleasure.
3. *Reading* is a pleasure.

In the first sentence, the action verb *read* takes the object *books*. In the second sentence, the action word *reading* takes the object *books*, and has the adverbial modifier *in the library*. It is therefore like a verb. It is also like a noun because it is subject of the verb *is*.

In the third sentence, *reading* is like a verb because it is an action word, and may be followed by an object or adverbial modifier. It is like a noun because it is subject of the verb *is*.

A word that has the value of a verb and a noun is called a VERBAL NOUN or GERUND.

EXERCISE 125

Select the gerunds and explain orally how each does the work of a verb and a noun.

1. Living here seems very pleasant.
2. Swimming is good exercise.
3. Making watches requires skilled workmen.
4. Eating too quickly gave him indigestion.
5. Tending my garden taught me many things about plants.
6. Splicing a rope is easy for a sailor.
7. Climbing mountains appears a dangerous sport.
8. Jumping over the fence is not easy.
9. Rising early is common in the country.
10. Skiing on the hills delighted the children.
11. Studying arithmetic was his favourite pastime.
12. Talking in the library is not permitted.
13. Pitching a ball develops muscle.

Gerunds as Objects and Subjective Completions

You have seen the gerund (or verbal noun) used as the subject of a sentence. It may also be used as the object of a verb or preposition, or as a subjective completion. Study the gerunds in italics in the following sentences:

1. I like *camping* beside a lake. (object of a verb)
2. He enjoys *picking* berries. (object of a verb)
3. He succeeds by *studying* hard. (object of a preposition)
4. She is skilful in *making* designs. (object of a preposition)
5. Seeing is *believing*. (subjective completion)
6. Acting is *imitating*. (subjective completion)

Use and Relation of Gerunds

The use and relation of a gerund should be given as follows:

Examples: We began *practising* our parts in the play.
Harmonizing is *singing* with others.

practising — a gerund. As a noun, it is object of the verb *began*; as a verb, it takes the object *parts*.

Harmonizing — a gerund. As a noun, it is subject of the verb *is*; as a verb, it expresses action.

singing — a gerund. As a noun, it is a subjective completion, completing the copula verb *is*; as a verb, it has the adverbial modifier *with others*.

EXERCISE 126

Give in writing the use and the relation of each gerund.

1. Did you have any difficulty in finding the way?
2. He earns extra money by delivering papers.
3. Shovelling coal is hard work.
4. I prefer waiting for a bus.
5. We intended going to the rink tonight.

6. Helping you is a pleasure.
7. He entertained his friends by showing pictures taken during his vacation.
8. She excels at introducing a speaker.
9. Mice destroy fruit trees by gnawing the bark.
10. I stopped playing in the orchestra.
11. I like studying astronomy.
12. Fretting never helps.

EXERCISE 127

Give orally the use and the relation of each gerund.

1. The children enjoy wading in the water.
2. He began his address by telling a story.
3. Collecting stamps is an interesting hobby.
4. This is the best time for catching trout.
5. We avoided the crowds by going early.
6. Shouting is not singing.
7. Playing hockey is a national sport.
8. Do you believe in practising immediately before a game?
9. Mending shoes is the work of a cobbler.
10. They gave him a medal for rescuing the child.
11. Walking in the country is pleasant exercise.
12. The debaters pleased the judges by speaking distinctly.
13. He tried teaching his dog a new trick.
14. Does travelling excel reading in increasing our knowledge of foreign lands?
15. I like getting letters, but I am not always prompt in answering them.
16. Making pastry is the work of a baker.
17. They tried turning the lock with a nail.
18. Many get pleasure from working among flowers.
19. Laughing is good for us.
20. We should learn the art of thinking.
21. Growing and selling vegetables is a profitable business.

Infinitives

Examine the words in italics in these sentences.

1. *Seeing* is *believing*.
2. *To see* is *to believe*.

You know that *seeing* and *believing* are gerunds, and that each has the value of a noun and a verb. Here they are replaced by *to see* and *to believe*, each of which must also have the value of a noun and a verb. Verb forms such as *to see* and *to believe*, which are used in the same way as gerunds, are called INFINITIVES.

Like a gerund, an infinitive may be the subject of a verb, the object of a verb, or a subjective completion; and it may take an object and have an adverbial modifier.

Examples: *To skate* well requires practice.
I intend *to go*.
To study is *to learn*.
We tried *to open* the door.
I learned *to type* at school.
Do not fail *to visit* the monument.

EXERCISE 128

Explain the use of each infinitive in the following sentences.

1. He soon learned to ride the bicycle.
2. To act on the stage is her ambition.
3. He likes to skate at the rink.
4. To reach a decision took only a moment.
5. He refused to work fast.
6. The girls wish to sit here.
7. To err is human.
8. I promised to go with him.
9. In the summer we plan to swim, to ride, and to rest.
10. He wanted to know your name.

Use and Relation of Infinitives

We give the use and relation of an infinitive just as we give the use and relation of a gerund.

Example: He wants *to see* the game.

To teach is *to instruct* someone.

to see — an infinitive. As a noun, it is object of the verb *wants*; as a verb, it takes the object *game*.

to teach — an infinitive. As a noun, it is subject of the verb *is*; as a verb, it expresses action.

to instruct — an infinitive. As a noun, it is a subjective completion, completing the verb *is*; as a verb, it takes the object *someone*.

EXERCISE 129

Give in writing the use and the relation of each infinitive.

1. To know him is to admire him.
2. They learned to sing many folk songs.
3. The boys offered to shovel the snow from our walk.
4. They decided to leave in the morning.
5. To look there never entered my mind.
6. She wants to consult a lawyer.
7. We mean to ask permission this evening.
8. They intend to visit Niagara Falls.
9. Do you wish to come with us?
10. To learn to pitch well is his greatest ambition.

EXERCISE 130

Give orally the use and the relation of each infinitive.

1. He wishes to start soon.
2. They endeavoured to launch the boat.
3. To understand that is easy.
4. I hope to know the result of the election tomorrow.
5. We managed to get there on time.
6. To blame him would be wrong.

7. They feared to leave the children alone.
8. To meet her is to like her.
9. Will you promise to write often?
10. He dreaded to face the stranger.
11. Try to swim without splashing.
12. He expects to rent his cottage for the summer.
13. To speak both English and French is a great advantage.
14. I plan to see him tomorrow.
15. Do not attempt to cross the street without looking in both directions.

Infinitives Used as Adjectives and Adverbs

In addition to the uses you have already learned, infinitives may have the value of adjectives or adverbs.

Examples: This is a book *to enjoy.*
Fools who came *to scoff* remained *to pray.*

The infinitive *to enjoy* in the first sentence describes *book*, and therefore has the value of an adjective, modifying *book*. The infinitive *to scoff* in the second sentence tells *why* they came, and therefore has the value of an adverb, modifying the verb *came*. Similarly, *to pray* has the value of an adverb because it tells *why* they remained.

When an infinitive is used in a sentence as an adjective or adverb, it appears to lose its value as a noun. This is not really the case, as you will see if you supply in such sentences the words that are understood. For example, the sentence *I came to see you* could be written *I came in order to see you*, since that is the meaning. Then the infinitive *to see* is object of the phrasal preposition *in order.*

148

The use of the infinitive as adjective or adverb should be given as follows:

Examples: He had a chance *to learn* a trade.

We ran *to catch* the train.

You are wise *to do* that.

to learn — an infinitive. As a verb, it takes the object *trade*; as an adjective, it modifies the noun *chance*.

to catch — an infinitive. As a verb, it takes the object *train*; as an adverb, it modifies the verb *ran*.

to do — an infinitive. As a verb, it takes the object *that*; as an adverb, it modifies the adjective *wise*.

Root Infinitives

To is called the sign of the infinitive. In some cases the sign *to* is omitted. Then the infinitive is called a ROOT INFINITIVE.

Examples: He does nothing but *read*. (to read)

I have seen him *do* that. (to do)

He bade us *enter*. (to enter)

You need not *leave* so soon. (to leave)

We watched the clouds *drift* by. (to drift)

EXERCISE 131

Give in writing the use and the relation of each infinitive.

1. We go to school to learn.
2. That was a day to remember.
3. They will come to visit us.
4. We did not have any wood to burn in the fireplace.
5. This is a machine to comb wool.
6. We went to meet our friends.
7. This is a good time to cut hay.
8. I am ready to leave.
9. We have not a minute to spare.
10. They stopped to inquire the way.

Give orally the use and the relation of each infinitive.

1. We decided to rise early.
2. To hold that position requires great ability.
3. Did you wish to have your vacation in July?
4. She needs to review her lessons more thoroughly.
5. He jumped high to catch the ball.
6. They agreed to sell the farm.
7. Now is the time to announce your decision.
8. We intend to succeed.
9. The children went to see the parade.
10. I hope to please my mother when I take home my report.
11. He dimmed his lights to assist the approaching cars.
12. To watch the bees was his delight.

Verbals

You have now studied three kinds of words formed from verbs. They are participles, gerunds, and infinitives. These are called VERBALS.

CHAPTER XVI

DIRECT AND INDIRECT OBJECTS

Direct and Indirect Objects

Read these sentences carefully, paying special attention to the words in italics.

1. He bought his *mother* a present.

2. They sent the *doctor* a telegram.

3. She made the *children* new coats.

4. Give *me* your pen.

In the first sentence, the verb *bought* appears to take two objects — *present* and *mother*. In the same way, in sentences 2, 3, and 4, the verbs appear to take two objects.

Suppose we look again at sentence 1, *He bought his mother a present.* This could be written: *He bought a present for his mother.* This has exactly the same meaning. With sentence 2, *They sent the doctor a telegram,* we could write: *They sent a telegram to the doctor.* Both sentences have the same meaning.

The last word in each of the four sentences listed above represents the thing toward which the action of the verb is directed. It is called the DIRECT OBJECT. The word in italics represents the person or thing the action is done *to* or *for*. It is called the INDIRECT OBJECT.

Notice that an indirect object always precedes a direct object in the same sentence.

Select the direct and indirect objects in each sentence.

1. He offered me his knife.
2. I told you his address.
3. His mother knitted him a warm sweater.
4. He gave his horse some feed.
5. The teacher read us a chapter of the book.
6. My father made me a boat.
7. Did you write her a letter?
8. They found him a position.
9. Please hand me the paper.
10. The usher gave me a good seat.
11. He told the judge his story.
12. The company pays its shareholders small dividends.
13. He willed his son the farm.
14. We gave the birds some crumbs.

Select the objects of verbs and tell whether they are direct or indirect.

1. Did he ask you the price of the coat?
2. We offered him a ride in our car.
3. He left the waiter a tip.
4. The boy gave the man a polite answer.
5. I chose her a gift.
6. She brought us some lunch.
7. He told them tales of his travels in Italy.
8. Your visit did him good.
9. The children took the sick woman a bouquet of flowers.
10. The messenger handed the policeman a telegram.
11. Have you told anyone our secret?
12. The successful inventor built his mother a comfortable house.
13. He gave the class a good report of the game.
14. Your answer gives me another idea.

CHAPTER XVII

ACTIVE AND PASSIVE VOICE
Active and Passive Voice, Progressive Tenses, Emphatic Tenses

Active and Passive Voice

Examine each pair of sentences to see how the same idea is expressed in two ways.

1. The boy *broke* the window.
   The window *was broken* by the boy.

2. My father *built* this house.
   This house *was built* by my father.

In the first sentence of each pair the verb expresses an action, and the subject names the *doer* of the action. In the second sentence of each pair the verb, in a changed form, expresses the same action, and the subject names the *receiver* of the action.

The change in the form of the verb to show whether the subject is the doer or the receiver of the action is called VOICE. When the subject indicates the doer of the action, the verb is said to be in the ACTIVE VOICE. When the subject indicates the receiver of the action, the verb is said to be in the PASSIVE VOICE.

EXERCISE 135

Tell whether the verb is in the active or passive voice.

1. The lifeguard rescued the child.
2. A board was torn off by the wind.
3. Blacksmiths shoe horses.

153

4. The dishes will be washed by the girls.
5. Piles of leaves were burned by the gardener.
6. The men praised the foreman.
7. Three trout were caught by my chum.
8. The robins ate the cherries.
9. The snow was melted by the sun.
10. The men moved the piano.
11. Did they mention it?
12. After the picnic they cleared up the litter.
13. The glass in the greenhouse was broken by the hailstones.
14. Henry and I cleaned the car.
15. The accident had not been reported by the motorist.

Changing from Active to Passive Voice

When you change the verb in a sentence from the active to the passive voice, the *object* in the active voice becomes the *subject* in the passive voice.

Examples: 1. The editor *wrote* the story. (Active Voice)
The story *was written* by the editor. (Passive Voice)
2. The hunter *noticed* tracks in the snow. (Active Voice)
Tracks in the snow *were noticed* by the hunter. (Passive Voice)

Notice that the passive voice is made up of the different forms of the verb *be* together with the past participle of the principal verb.

Since only transitive verbs can have objects, it is apparent that only transitive verbs can be changed to the passive voice.

Note: The word that shows the doer of the action is often omitted in the passive voice.

Example: I found the purse. (Active)
The purse was found. (Passive)

(a) Write out each sentence, changing the verbs from active to passive, and from passive to active. Make sure that the tense of the verb remains the same.

1. The engineer quickly stopped the train.
2. Many rabbits are killed by wolves.
3. Robert will represent our school at the meeting.
4. The landlord notified the tenant to leave.
5. Every year the farmer taps the sugar-maple trees.
6. Much sediment is carried by rivers.
7. These posters were made by senior pupils.
8. Our examination results will be published in the newspaper.
9. The sightseers are being conducted by a guide.
10. Several books of travel were ordered by the librarian.
11. The policeman caught the thief.
12. More freight is now transported by plane than ten years ago.
13. The driver applied his brakes.
14. The corn was damaged by the frost.
15. We reached the summit at twilight.

(b) Change orally from active to passive, and from passive to active.

1. The men cleared the wreckage from the track.
2. The boy directed the stranger.
3. The drought was ended by a heavy rain.
4. The people were waked by the barking of their dog.
5. In the fall the farmer fills his silo with corn.
6. Old trails through the forest were made by the Indians.
7. You will disappoint your parents.
8. The carpenter shingled the roof of the house.
9. A good watchmaker repaired my watch.
10. I opened the door very carefully.
11. The crops were damaged by the storm.
12. I have told that story many times.

Conjugation in the Passive Voice

You learned how to conjugate verbs in six tenses in the active voice. (Pages 65 and 71.) Here you are shown the conjugation of the verb *see* in the passive voice.

PRESENT TENSE

	Singular	*Plural*
1st Person	I am seen	we are seen
2nd Person	you are seen	you are seen
3rd Person	he is seen	they are seen

PAST TENSE

	Singular	*Plural*
1st Person	I was seen	we were seen
2nd Person	you were seen	you were seen
3rd Person	he was seen	they were seen

FUTURE TENSE

	Singular	*Plural*
1st Person	I shall be seen	we shall be seen
2nd Person	you will be seen	you will be seen
3rd Person	he will be seen	they will be seen

PRESENT PERFECT TENSE

	Singular	*Plural*
1st Person	I have been seen	we have been seen
2nd Person	you have been seen	you have been seen
3rd Person	he has been seen	they have been seen

PAST PERFECT TENSE

	Singular	*Plural*
1st Person	I had been seen	we had been seen
2nd Person	you had been seen	you had been seen
3rd Person	he had been seen	they had been seen

FUTURE PERFECT TENSE

	Singular	*Plural*
1st Person	I shall have been seen	we shall have been seen
2nd Person	you will have been seen	you will have been seen
3rd Person	he will have been seen	they will have been seen

(a) In the active voice, write the conjugation of the verbs *tell* and *know* in the present, past, and future tenses.
(b) In the passive voice, write the conjugation of the verbs *tell* and *know* in the present, past, and future tenses.

(a) In the active voice, write the conjugation of the verbs *hear* and *hurt* in the three perfect tenses.
(b) In the passive voice, write the conjugation of the verbs *hear* and *hurt* in the three perfect tenses.

(a) In the active voice give orally the conjugation of the verbs *teach* and *show* in the six tenses.
(b) In the passive voice, give orally the conjugation of the verbs *teach* and *show* in the six tenses.

(a) In the active voice give orally the conjugation of verbs *help* and *praise* in the six tenses.
(b) In the passive voice, give orally the conjugation of verbs *help* and *praise* in the six tenses.

Write the following tense forms of the verb *choose*:

    i. third person singular, past tense, passive voice
   ii. second person plural, future perfect tense, passive voice
  iii. first person plural, present perfect tense, passive voice
  iv. third person plural, past perfect tense, passive voice
   v. second person singular, present tense, passive voice
  vi. third person singular, future perfect tense, passive voice
 vii. third person singular, future tense, passive voice
viii. first person plural, present tense, passive voice

Give orally the following tense forms of the verb *help*:

   i. first person singular, present tense, passive voice
  ii. third person singular, past tense, passive voice
 iii. third person plural, future tense, passive voice
 iv. second person singular, present perfect tense, passive voice
  v. first person plural, past tense, passive voice
 vi. second person plural, past perfect tense, passive voice
vii. third person plural, past perfect tense, passive voice
viii. third person singular, future perfect tense, passive voice
 ix. second person singular, future tense, passive voice
  x. first person singular, present perfect tense, passive voice
 xi. third person plural, present tense, passive voice
xii. first person plural, present perfect tense, passive voice

Write the following tense forms of the verb *pay*:

   i. third person singular, present tense, active voice
  ii. third person plural, past perfect tense, passive voice
 iii. first person singular, past tense, active voice
 iv. second person plural, future tense, passive voice
  v. first person plural, past perfect tense, passive voice
 vi. third person plural, future tense, active voice
vii. first person plural, future perfect tense, passive voice
viii. third person singular, past perfect tense, active voice
 ix. second person singular, present perfect tense, passive voice
  x. third person singular, future tense, active voice
 xi. first person singular, past perfect tense, active voice
xii. first person plural, present tense, active voice

Progressive Tenses — Active and Passive

Study the following sentences, paying particular attention to the tense and form of each verb:

1. I *am watching* you.
2. I *was watching* you.
3. I *shall be watching* you.

Here the verb phrase indicates an action as going on at the time shown by the tense of the verb. It is a *continuing action* at that time. A continuing action is shown by a PROGRESSIVE TENSE of the verb.

The progressive tenses of the verb *watch* shown above are the present, past, and future. There are also PERFECT PROGRESSIVE TENSES.

Examples:

I *have been watching.* (present perfect progressive)
I *had been watching.* (past perfect progressive)
I *shall have been watching.* (future perfect progressive)

All the progressive tenses given above are in the active voice.. In the passive voice, we find progressive tenses in the present and past only.

Examples:

I *am being watched.* (present progressive tense, passive voice)

I *was being watched.* (past progressive tense, passive voice)

Notice that in the active voice, progressive tenses are formed by using the present participle of the principal verb with different forms of the verb *be.* In the passive voice, the two progressive tenses are formed by using the past participle of the principal verb, preceded by   word *being,* with the present and past forms of the verb *be.*

Conjugation in Progressive Tenses

You are given here the first person, singular and plural, for each progressive tense, active voice; and for the two progressive tenses in the passive voice, of the verb *tell*.

ACTIVE VOICE

	Singular	Plural
Present Progressive:	I am telling	we are telling
Past Progressive:	I was telling	we were telling
Future Progressive:	I shall be telling	we shall be telling
Present Perfect Progressive:	I have been telling	we have been telling
Past Perfect Progressive:	I had been telling	we had been telling
Future Perfect Progressive:	I shall have been telling	we shall have been telling

PASSIVE VOICE

	Singular	Plural
Present Progressive:	I am being told	we are being told
Past Progressive:	I was being told	we were being told

(a) Write in full the conjugation of the verb *tell* in the six progressive tenses, active voice. For your model, use the conjugation of the verb *see* on another page.

(b) Write the conjugation of the verb *tell* in the present and past progressive tenses, passive voice.

(a) Give orally the conjugation of the verb *watch* in the six progressive tenses, active voice.

(b) Give orally the conjugation of the verb *watch* in the present and past progressive tenses, passive voice.

Write the following tense forms of the verb *give*:

    i. third person singular, present progressive, active voice

    ii. first person plural, future progressive, active voice

    iii. second person singular, past perfect progressive, active voice

    iv. first person singular, future perfect progressive, active voice

    v. third person plural, past progressive, active voice

    vi. second person plural, present perfect progressive, active voice

    vii. first person singular, present progressive, active voice

    viii. third person singular, future progressive, active voice

    ix. third person plural, past perfect progressive, active voice

    x. first person plural, past progressive, active voice

    xi. first person singular, present tense, passive voice

    xii. third person plural, past tense, passive voice

    xiii. second person plural, present tense, passive voice

    xiv. third person singular, present tense, passive voice

    xv. first person plural, past tense, passive voice

Emphatic Tenses

Examine the verbs in these sentences.

1. He *lives* there.   2. I *gave* it to you.
   He *does live* there.   I *did give* it to you.

In the first sentence of each pair, the verb simply *asserts*. In the second sentence of each pair, the verb *asserts emphatically*. The emphasis is shown by the use of the words *do* and *did*. These auxiliaries help the principal verb to form an EMPHATIC TENSE.

Emphatic tenses are found in the present and past only. Here are the emphatic tenses of the verb *think*.

PRESENT EMPHATIC TENSE

	Singular	*Plural*
1st Person	I do think	we do think
2nd Person	you do think	you do think
3rd Person	he does think	they do think

PAST EMPHATIC TENSE

	Singular	*Plural*
1st Person	I did think	we did think
2nd Person	you did think	you did think
3rd Person	he did think	they did think

It should be noted that, in addition to its use as an auxiliary verb in emphatic tenses, *do* is used as an auxiliary in questions and in negative statements, and in the imperative.

Examples: Where *do* you live? Why *did* he leave?
     I *do* not wish to go. We *did* not see them.
     Do stay!

Note also that *do* may be used as a principal verb.

Examples: You *do* better than you think.
     He *does* his work neatly.
     They *did* well to come.

Conjugate each of the following verbs in the present emphatic and past emphatic tenses:

sing, work, study, try, play

CHAPTER XVIII

GENERAL REVIEW

REVIEW—Nouns

REVIEW EXERCISE 1

From the following sentences select orally the nouns, giving the kind, number, case, and relation of each:

1. Newfoundland is Canada's tenth province.
2. When Cartier sailed across the Atlantic in 1543, he was not crossing unknown seas.
3. Television is a scientific achievement that will provide entertainment for the millions.
4. Mount Vesuvius towers above the city of Naples.
5. The directors' signatures are on the promissory note.
6. Several of Norway's modern ships were purchased from other countries.
7. The fourth of July is a national holiday in the United States.
8. Richard's eyes sparkled with indignation, but his better nature quickly overcame it. He pressed his hand against his brow and studied the face of the humbled baron, in whose features pride and shame were contending.

REVIEW—Pronouns

REVIEW EXERCISE 2

Give orally the kind, person, number, case, and relation of each pronoun.

1. They made room for us in their car.
2. I left my coat on the bench.
3. Everyone but me has a new hat.
4. Who will help me to mow the lawn?
5. He and I went together.
6. Several praised him for his speech.
7. You are taller than he.
8. For whom are you waiting?

9. She and he are friends.
10. Who stood beside me?
11. I knew that you went with them.
12. We invited him for dinner.
13. That is she at the desk.
14. John and he are cousins.
15. We saw him and his sister at the game.
16. These are hardy rose-bushes.
17. Everybody knew where you had gone.
18. For whom did you vote?
19. I do not know the boy whom you spoke to.
20. He does not sing as well as she.
21. He is a better player than I.
22. We could not find the man who owned the car.

REVIEW—Correct Usage of Pronouns

REVIEW EXERCISE 3

Write out each sentence, using the correct word from the pair given in brackets. Be prepared to give the reason for your choice.

1. I am older than (she, her).
2. (Who, whom) is the guilty one?
3. He said that you and (me, I) might go.
4. They should not blame (we, us).
5. He is younger than (I, me).
6. We waited for you and (him, he).
7. (Who, whom) did the teacher call?
8. You skate as well as (me, I).
9. I think it was (her, she).
10. You and (I, me) were in the same class.
11. No one except (he, him) would do that.
12. You work faster than (I, me).
13. They saw you and (I, me) together.
14. Did you think it was (him, he)?
15. (Who, whom) are you going with?
16. People like (she, her) need plenty of sleep.
17. (Who, whom) did you tell?

165

18. This seat is good enough for you and (me, I).
19. We met (they, them) at the corner.
20. They are friends (whom, who) I seldom see.

REVIEW—Classes of Verbs

REVIEW EXERCISE 4

Classify the verbs as transitive, intransitive, or copula.

1. The boys were playing games in the yard.
2. The weather suddenly turned cold.
3. She seems contented.
4. I did not believe the report.
5. Most children sleep soundly.
6. He became a great musician.
7. The woman prepared the dinner in a hurry.
8. The sick child grew nervous during the storm.
9. Birds generally build their nests in sheltered places.
10. The snow never melts on the peaks of some mountains.
11. I was very happy after the game.
12. He has been away for a month.
13. These cakes taste good.
14. Do you feel dizzy?
15. He opens his letters with a penknife.
16. The story sounded mysterious to me.
17. He walked hurriedly away.
18. We were on the ship for three days.
19. The boys found some old coins in the cave.
20. The boat looks safe.
21. He is a very capable workman.
22. The teacher did not see us.

REVIEW—Agreement between Subject and Predicate

REVIEW EXERCISE 5

Use the correct word from the pair given in brackets, and be prepared to give the reason for your choice.

1. Clouds continually................through the sky. (pass, passes)
2. Many varieties of the palm-tree................found in tropical countries. (is, are)
3. He........ ....eat much meat. (don't, doesn't)

166

4. They................at the museum yesterday. (was, were)
5. Every pupil in our class................that the examination was difficult. (think, thinks)
6. There................a good supply of vegetables on the market. (was, were)
7. The members of the council often................. (disagrees, disagree)
8. All the companies in our town................good wages. (pay, pays)
9. The man and the woman................crossing the street. (was, were)
10. There................too many people in this room. (is, are)
11. Here................the boy and his sister. (comes, come)
12. ....there any vacant seats? (was, were)
13. The white lines on the curves in the road................accidents. (prevent, prevents)
14. There................to be particles of sand in the spinach. (seem, seems)
15. ....you late for dinner today? (were, was)
16. One of my friends................to that school. (go, goes)
17. The hunter and his dogs................crossing the field. (are, is)
18. ....there anyone in our class who failed? (were, was)
19. This is one of the houses that................sold. (was, were)
20. Many who work in this factory................in the country. (lives, live)
21. The names of the members of the committee................not published. (was, were)
22. Not one of my answers................correct. (is, are)
23. ....there many at the game? (was, were)
24. The farmer and his neighbours................doing the work. (are, is)

REVIEW—Conjugation of Verbs

REVIEW EXERCISE 6

(a) Conjugate the verb *begin* in the present, past, and future tenses.

(b) Conjugate the verb *eat* in the present perfect, past perfect, and future perfect tenses.

(c) Conjugate the verb *study* in the six tenses.

Give orally the following tense forms of the verb *come*:

    i. second person plural, future tense
    ii. third person singular, past tense
   iii. first person plural, present tense
   iv. third person plural, past perfect tense
    v. first person singular, future tense
   vi. third person plural, future perfect tense
  vii. first person plural, present perfect tense
 viii. third person plural, future tense
   ix. third person singular, present tense
    x. second person singular, past perfect tense

REVIEW—Correct Usage of Verbs

REVIEW EXERCISE 8

Write out each sentence, using the correct word from the pair given in brackets.

1. Have you (*give, given*) your oral composition yet?
2. I (*saw, seen*) your brother at church yesterday.
3. That horse has (*ran, run*) on this track before.
4. I know you (*done, did*) your job well.
5. The ships have (*went, gone*) out with the tide.
6. They have (*known, knew*) each other for a long time.
7. She had never (*saw, seen*) the ocean before.
8. We (*come, came*) home yesterday.
9. The boys have (*went, gone*) for a Christmas tree.
10. He has never (*done, did*) that kind of work.
11. I (*give, gave*) him my hockey-stick for the game.
12. They (*begun, began*) to drill the new well today.
13. Who (*sung, sang*) in the choir on Sunday?
14. Have you (*seen, saw*) a robin yet?
15. Several pupils have (*written, wrote*) long letters.
16. They have (*took, taken*) the flag down.
17. Has the teacher (*rung, rang*) the bell?
18. This wheat has (*grew, grown*) fast.
19. It (*begin, began*) to rain in the night.

20. They (*done, did*) us a favour.
21. I have (*drove, driven*) a car for a long time.
22. He (*give, gave*) away most of his money.
23. I have never (*ate, eaten*) here before.
24. We (*drunk, drank*) from a wooden cup.
25. He (*sit, sat*) in the same spot again today.

REVIEW—Correct Usage of Adjectives and Adverbs

REVIEW EXERCISE 9

Write out each sentence, using the correct word from the pair given in brackets.

1. The hungry man looked............... ....at the food. (eager, eagerly)
2. The woman feels........................in her own home. (happy, happily)
3. Try to act................with strangers. (natural, naturally)
4. Your plans look.................to me. (well, good)
5. He appeared................to leave. (anxious, anxiously)
6. The child does not talk................. (clear, clearly)
7. You were................fortunate today. (sure, surely)
8. They are not..... ....ready. (near, nearly)
9. She skates very...... .... (graceful, gracefully)
10. You have done this work...... .. .. (good, well)
11. That horse won the race... .... (easily, easy)
12. The flowers smell.... .. .. (sweetly, sweet)
13. Several guests felt......... ......after eating the food. (queerly, queer)
14. The doctor says that the boy is not.......... ...... (good, well)
15. How................the child looks! (prettily, pretty)
16. The boy spoke................to his employer. (politely, polite)
17. He waited................for news from his son. (anxious, anxiously)
18. Food tastes................when we are hungry. (good, well)
19. He spoke very................. (disagreeable, disagreeably)
20. I felt................when I heard you were coming. (well, good)
21. That news sounds................ (well, good)
22. He looked................after his operation. (bad, badly)

REVIEW—Different Uses of the Same Word

(a) Compose sentences using each of the following words as a noun. Then compose sentences using each word as a verb.

plant, place, mark, watch, search

(b) Use each word as a preposition and an adverb.

in, near, up, past, above

(c) Use each word as an adjective and an adverb.

early, back, right, first, only

(d) Use each word as a noun, a verb, and an adjective.

light, equal, sound, work, open

(e) Use each word as a preposition and a conjunction.

after, for, until, before, since

REVIEW—Clauses

(a) Write a sentence with a noun clause as the subject of the verb.

(b) Write a sentence with a noun clause as the object of the verb.

(c) Write a complex sentence which contains a principal clause, an adjective clause, and an adverb clause.

(d) Write a complex sentence which contains a principal clause, an adjective clause, an adverb clause, and a noun clause.

(e) Write a compound-complex sentence.

REVIEW—Clauses and Relation of Words

(a) In the following extract select all the clauses, and give the kind and relation of each subordinate clause.

(b) Give orally the part of speech and the relation or use of each word.

In the heat of the action, as he advanced at the head of the grenadiers of Louisburg, a bullet shattered his wrist, but he wrapped his handkerchief about the wound, and showed no sign of pain.

REVIEW—Clauses

In the following stanzas select all the clauses, and give the kind and the relation of each subordinate clause.

1.   Sadly, as the shades of even
       Gathered o'er the hill,
       While the western half of heaven
       Blushed with sunset still,
       From the fountain's mossy seat
       Turned the Indian's weary feet.

2.   The curfew tolls the knell of parting day,
       The lowing herd winds slowly o'er the lea,
       The ploughman homeward plods his weary way,
       And leaves the world to darkness and to me.

3.   When I was a beggarly boy
           And lived in a cellar damp,
       I had not a friend or a toy,
           But I had Aladdin's lamp;
       When I could not sleep for cold,
           I had fire enough in my brain,
       And builded with roofs of gold
           My beautiful castles in Spain!

REVIEW—Clauses

In the following extracts select all the clauses, and give the kind and the relation of each subordinate clause.

1. Tom was sitting at the bottom of his bed unlacing his boots, so that his back was toward Arthur, and he did not see what had happened, and looked up in wonder at the sudden silence.

2. When I was a little advanced into the island I saw an old man, who appeared very weak and infirm. He was sitting on the bank of a stream, and at first I took him to be one who had been shipwrecked like myself. I went towards him and saluted him, but he only slightly bowed his head.

3. I had been often told that the rock before me was the haunt of a genius; and that several had been entertained with music who had passed by it, but never heard that the musician had before made himself visible.

REVIEW—Verbals

Give the kind, use, and relation of each verbal.

1. Flying a kite requires a steady breeze.
2. Tangled and broken, the wires lay on the street.
3. To hitch one's wagon to a star means to plan ambitiously.
4. Skating at top speed, he outdistanced all his competitors.
5. We enjoyed listening to the symphony concert.
6. Having gone out in a hurry, he forgot his coat.
7. A boy went by, whistling a lively tune.
8. The children picked flowers growing along the road.
9. To eat too much candy is a mistake.
10. They asked us to paint the house.
11. We saw people strolling in the park.
12. He enjoys discussing politics.
13. The children planned to surprise their mother with a gift.
14. I was glad to meet her.
15. To remember names is easy for some.
16. She went out to get a magazine.
17. Letters dropped in this mailbox are collected late at night.
18. Having come so far, we want to get a seat for the game.
19. Snow drifting across the highway blocked traffic.
20. Trees uprooted by the hurricane lay on every side.
21. That is a plane to carry freight.
22. He determined to outwit the enemy.
23. Having been hurt in the game, he was limping badly.
24. Tents pitched by the Boy Scouts soon covered the field.
25. This is the mine discovered by the trapper.
26. Having read the book, I enjoyed the motion-picture.
27. Sewing in a poor light is not a good practice.
28. She pleased him by admiring his pony.

REVIEW—Direct and Indirect Objects

(a) Write three sentences in which a pronoun is the object of a preposition.

(b) Write three sentences in which a noun is the object of a preposition.

(c) Write three sentences in which a noun or pronoun is the direct object of a verb.

(d) Write three sentences in which a noun or pronoun is the indirect object of a verb.

REVIEW—Verbs: Active and Passive Voice

REVIEW EXERCISE 17

(a) Conjugate the verb *think* in the six regular tenses, active voice.

(b) Conjugate the verb *send* in the six regular tenses, passive voice.

REVIEW—Verbs: Progressive Tenses

REVIEW EXERCISE 18

(a) Conjugate the verb *show* in the six progressive tenses, active voice.

(b) Conjugate the verb *hear* in the present progressive and past progressive tenses, passive voice.

REVIEW—Verbs: Emphatic Tenses

REVIEW EXERCISE 19

Conjugate each verb in the present emphatic and past emphatic tenses:

> believe, learn, help, drive, buy

APPENDIX

Gender Nouns, Principal Parts of Verbs, Foreign Word
Plurals, Comparison of Adjectives

A — Gender Nouns

Masculine	Feminine	Masculine	Feminine
abbot	abbess	husband	wife
author	author *or*	king	queen
	authoress	lad	lass
bachelor	spinster	landlord	landlady
	or maid	lord	lady
beau	belle	master	mistress
billy-goat	nanny-goat	monk	nun
or he-goat	*or* she-goat	nephew	niece
boy	girl	poet	poet
bridegroom	bride		*or* poetess
buck	doe	prophet	prophetess
cock	hen	ram	ewe
colt	filly	shepherd	shepherdess
drake	duck	son	daughter
duke	duchess	stag	hind
emperor	empress	uncle	aunt
fox	vixen	waiter	waitress
gander	goose	widower	widow
gentleman	lady	youth	maiden

B — Principal Parts of Verb

Present Tense	Past Tense	Past Participle
arise	arose	arisen
awake	awoke	awoke *or* awaked
bear	bore	borne
bid	bade *or* bid	bidden *or* bid
bind	bound	bound
bite	bit	bitten
blow	blew	blown
burst	burst	burst
buy	bought	bought
catch	caught	caught
choose	chose	chosen
climb	climbed	climbed
dive	dived	dived
drink	drank	drunk
fight	fought	fought
find	found	found
forget	forgot	forgotten
forsake	forsook	forsaken
freeze	froze	frozen
grind	ground	ground
hang	hanged	hanged
	(of person in capital punishment)	
hang	hung	hung
	(of thing or person in all other cases)	
hide	hid	hidden
hold	held	held
mow	mowed	mowed *or* mown
prove	proved	proved
ride	rode	ridden

176

Present Tense	Past Tense	Past Participle
sew	sewed	sewn *or* sewed
shine	shone	shone
sow	sowed	sown *or* sowed
speak	spoke	spoken
strive	strove	striven
swim	swam	swum
swing	swung	swung
wake	woke *or* waked	waked, woke *or* woken
weave	wove	woven
work	worked *or* wrought	worked *or* wrought

C — Plurals of Some Foreign Words

Singular	Plural
analysis	analyses
appendix	appendices
axis	axes
bandit	bandits *or* banditti
crisis	crises
formula	formulas *or* formulæ
index	indexes *or* indices
medium	media
memorandum	memorandums *or* memoranda
parenthesis	parentheses
vertebra	vertebræ

D — Comparison of Adjectives

Positive	Comparative	Superlative
angry	angrier	angriest
busy	busier	busiest
careful	more careful	most careful
common	commoner	commonest
eager	more eager	most eager
earnest	more earnest	most earnest
easy	easier	easiest
fearful	more fearful	most fearful
healthy	healthier	healthiest
lively	livelier	liveliest
lovely	lovelier	loveliest
sultry	sultrier	sultriest
ugly	uglier	ugliest
unkind	unkinder	unkindest
worldly	more worldly	most worldly
worthy	worthier	worthiest

GENERAL INDEX